The Changing Sixth Form in the Twentieth Century

The Changing Sixth Form in the Twentieth Century

by A. D. Edwards

*Lecturer in Education,
University of Exeter*

LONDON
ROUTLEDGE & KEGAN PAUL
NEW YORK : HUMANITIES PRESS

First published 1970
by Routledge & Kegan Paul Ltd
Broadway House, 68-74 Carter Lane
London E.C.4
Printed in Great Britain
by Northumberland Press Limited
Gateshead-on-Tyne
SBN 7100 6742 9 (c)
SBN 7100 6743 7 (p)

THE STUDENTS LIBRARY OF EDUCATION has been designed to meet the needs of students of Education at Colleges of Education and at University Institutes and Departments. It will also be valuable for practising teachers and educationists. The series takes full account of the latest developments in teacher-training and of new methods and approaches in education. Separate volumes will provide authoritative and up-to-date accounts of the topics within the major fields of sociology, philosophy and history of education, educational psychology, and method. Care has been taken that specialist topics are treated lucidly and usefully for the non-specialist reader. Altogether, the Students' Library of Education will provide a comprehensive introduction and guide to anyone concerned with the study of education and with educational theory and practice.

J. W. TIBBLE

Between 1955 and 1965 the numbers of sixth formers doubled. With the extension of comprehensive education, those staying on at school for a sixth or seventh year will not be confined only to those who were selected for grammar schools. There is likely, therefore, to be further massive increases in the future. What kind of organization is required to meet this demand? The 'new' sixth form in the comprehensive school? One or other variant of the sixth-form college? The sixth-form centre? And what should be the content of education at this stage?

These are important questions on which our thinking is clearly influenced by past experience and practice. Mr. Edwards gives a concise history of the sixth form, and discusses historical influences that have determined its growth and character from the first decades of this century. This book compliments Eric Eaglesham's *Foundations of 20th-Century Education in England*, and might be read in conjunction with it.

B.SIMON

Contents

Introduction

Through all the educational changes of this century, there has been a remarkable continuity in ideas about the work and purpose of the grammar school sixth form. The value of 'this most precious jewel in the crown of English secondary education' has been defined as a rigorous intellectual training through academic study, and a sound character training through active participation in the running of a school. Nowhere else has school work been so specialized and intensive. Nowhere else have senior pupils been so deliberately 'trained to lead'. The main function of the sixth form has long been accepted as the preparation of the academically inclined for university study or professional training. It has therefore represented at its most effective the grammar schools' 'lift or stairway to the highest storeys of the social structure'.

Such ideas of the sixth form owe much to the public schools and the large, endowed grammar schools of the last century, and the famous description in the Crowther Report borrows heavily from the past. Sixth forms are linked closely to the universities and feed the specialist interests and 'subject-mindedness' of their pupils. There is a relationship of 'intellectual discipleship' between teacher

x

and taught, a relationship which implies small numbers and a common taste for academic study. The place of the sixth form as a source of standards in work and behaviour to the rest of the school provides an invaluable training in social responsibility. This high theory was followed by the question—'Is a sixth form in this sense to be regarded as a luxury of the past . . . ?' (Crowther, 1959, 225). It is the impact of rapidly growing numbers and new needs on traditional assumptions about the sixth form which provides the main theme of this book. The focus throughout is on the state system, not the independent schools, and until the 1950s this meant sixth forms in grammar schools. The recent development of radically different approaches to 'upper secondary schooling' make necessary the much wider perspective of the last chapter.

Dr. George Baron of the London University Institute of Education gave me great help and encouragement in my original research on the sixth form. My colleague, Mr. C. P. Hill, kindly read most of the manuscript of this book, removing many errors of fact and style without being in any way responsible for those that stubbornly remain. I am also most grateful for the experience and enjoyment of sixth-form teaching at East Ham Grammar School and Latymer Upper School, and for many discussions with colleagues there on the problems of such work.

Abbreviations

The following abbreviations are used in the text:

A.M.A.—*Journal of the Incorporated Association of Assistant Masters*

B.E.—Board of Education Circular, Report or Statistics

H.M.A.—Headmasters' Association

H.R.—*Headmasters' Review*, Journal of the Incorporated Association of Headmasters

H.U.C.—Home Universities Conference

I.A.A.M.—Incorporated Association of Assistant Masters

J.E.—*Journal of Education*

S.S.E.C.—Secondary School Examinations Council

T.E.S.—*Times Educational Supplement*

U.C.C.A.—Universities' Central Council on Admissions

U.G.C.—University Grants Committee

U.Q.—*Universities Quarterly*

1

A thin topsoil of advanced work, 1900-1920

The sixth form at Rugby School was described by a pupil of Thomas Arnold as 'an aristocracy of talent and worth . . . an organized and responsible nobility' (Briggs, 1965, 164). Arnold built up the power and privileges of his sixth form, seeing a vital means of discipline and moral influence in what he called 'the peculiar relationship of the highest form to the rest of the boys such as exists in our great public schools'. He made use of the traditional independence of the older boys, turning them from rebel leaders into junior officers and so curbing the disorder common before his time. And he took a special pride in his success —'When I have the confidence of the sixth, there is no post in England I would exchange for this'. Despite the Arnold legend, however, his methods were not unique. Sixth forms developed strongly in the 'great' schools, offering those on the edge of the universities a chance to lead and take responsibility, and to concentrate on a few chosen subjects. But in most nineteenth-century grammar schools, advanced work was sparse or non-existent. They struggled to provide courses for pupils who often left at 15 or earlier, with sixth-form work often a matter of individual tuition in a teacher's free time.

Advanced work in schools in 1900

The enormous range of secondary schools is shown very clearly in the Bryce Report of 1895, where they are classified according to the leaving age and future occupations of their pupils. At the top were those first-grade schools 'whose special function is the creation of a learned or literary, and a professional or cultural class . . . the class whose school life continues till 18 or 19, and would naturally end in the universities' (Bryce, i. 138). Their academic record was often formidable. The Manchester Grammar School was sending fifty pupils a year to university in the 1890s, and Bristol Grammar School's 'reputation for scholarship' had brought local protests at the sacrifice of the many to the exceptionally able. St. Paul's School was then winning more open awards at Oxford and Cambridge than any other two schools together, and the young Compton Mackenzie was soon to rebel against its scholarship hunting—'I had too many passionate interests to feel that the object of one's existence should be scholastic honour and glory for a school' (Mackenzie, 1963, 216).

These were exceptional schools in size, resources, the recruitment of able pupils and staff, and in their close links with Oxford and Cambridge. Only eight of Yorkshire's thirty-six grammar schools, for example, were found worthy of this first division. Far more numerous were the second-grade schools. While they might send a few pupils to the local university, their main function was 'the education of men with a view to some form of commercial or industrial life'. A little culture was not excluded, but most of their pupils would go 'straight into the work of life' at the age of 16 (Bryce, i. 141). The limited scope and ambition of many such schools around the turn of the century is described in the surveys of secondary education carried out

2

for several local authorities by Michael Sadler. His report on Essex, for example, is full of regrets at 'so little connection with the universities'. Where there was such a connection it brought proud comments from headmasters and was paraded in prospectuses.

Some grammar schools were placed with the Higher-Grade schools in a third category 'whose special function is the training of boys and girls for the higher handicrafts, or the commerce of the shop and town' (Bryce, i. 142). But to complicate still further the already confused relationship between elementary and secondary education, a few higher-grade schools stepped beyond these limits, continuing the education of their best pupils 'for some time after the age of 15, preparing them for a scholarship competition, or for Matriculation at the local University College or at the University of London'. Working within the elementary code, the Nottingham School Board allowed its top standard to study French, German and Latin, and to prepare for university local examinations, while the Leeds Higher Grade Schools had sixteen boys over the age of 17 in 1894, most of whom were going on directly to the University College.

Such trespassing on the grammar schools' territory brought protests, and demands for an upper limit on the education offered by board schools. A maximum leaving age of 15 was duly announced in 1900. But very few school boards could offer these 'dangerous' opportunities for prolonged schooling, and only a tiny minority of elementary school children stayed beyond the age of 14. What was disturbing was the number of grammar school pupils who stayed no longer. Some had no choice, being in schools little more than Higher Elementary in what they could offer. Even second-grade schools found difficulty in providing more than a 'thin topsoil of advanced work'. Yet a distinguished headmistress described 'the sixth form' as 'that phrase laden with associations of dignity and weight to an English boy or girl' (Burstall, 1907, 36). To her own pupils, these associations may well have been strong. But in the ordinary grammar school around 1900, 'that phrase' meant very little.

The Education Act of 1902

The School Boards were finally warned off the field of secondary education by the Cockerton Judgment of 1900. Two years later, they were swept away altogether, and it was the county and county borough councils which were to—'supply, or aid the supply of, education other than elementary'. They could either build new secondary schools of their own, or aid the endowed schools of their area. Much was left to their initiative, and an Act which gave plenty of scope to energetic authorities gave little power to compel the laggards. The need to expand secondary education was widely accepted. The superiority of the German education system was causing alarm. So were the low educational standards of many teachers, and it was announced in 1907 that those intending to teach were to continue their education in secondary schools rather than in pupil-teacher centres. In 1905 there were 95,000 children in the grant-aided secondary schools of England and Wales. That number had risen to 158,000 by 1910, and to 308,000 by 1920.

The obvious effect of this expansion on advanced work was to broaden the base from which it grew. So many grammar schools before 1902 had been crippled by lack of numbers and lack of money. They were sometimes crippled still further by competition from Higher-Grade schools housed in new buildings and offering a wider range of courses. Now these either became secondary schools of the normal kind or were placed firmly back at the elementary level. Aid from the rates became available to those grammar schools willing to accept some loss of independence and receive a somewhat wider social intake. And by 1914 over 300 new secondary schools had been built by local authorities, often as fervent expressions of civic pride or egalitarian purpose.

The continued inadequacy of sixth-form work

1. Early leaving

The Free Place Regulations of 1907 restricted aid from public funds to grammar schools which made themselves 'accessible to all classes' by taking 25 per cent of their intake from elementary schools. There were immediate fears that standards would fall. Surely there was not 'sufficient material' in the elementary schools to fill those places? School work would suffer from 'lack of culture in the home', and there was a grave risk of exploiting the grammar schools for the sake of a working class 'which does not appreciate the privilege, and which abuses it in a most impudent way' (*J.E.*, August 1902; *A.M.A.*, July 1909, 64).

Complaints died away as teachers realized that those with free places tended to stay longer and to do rather better in examinations. This was not really surprising, for these pupils tended to be the intellectual and social elite of their schools. Though the Board of Education described the free place examinations as qualifying and not competitive, its good intentions collapsed beneath the fierce demand for places. And since middle-class parents were gradually making more use of the elementary schools, their children

5

were particularly successful in this competition. By 1915 almost a third of grammar school places were free, and filled by pupils able to cope with, and normally committed to, a full secondary course. Indeed, local authorities began to ask for guarantees that they *would* stay long enough to justify scholarships which were, after all, 'investments, not a form of charity'. This social investment side of the scholarship system was especially obvious in those bursaries offered to intending teachers which allowed 'uninterrupted attendance' at a secondary school 'until the age of 17 or 18'. Open to attack as bribes and a way of avoiding a decent starting salary, they did keep at school many thousands who would previously have been instructed part-time in pupil-teacher centres.

These changes increased the average length of secondary school life. But what Michael Sadler wrote of one school in 1904 remained generally true, that 'the unwillingness of parents, "heedless of far gain", to allow their sons to remain the full four years of a secondary curriculum is all against the maintenance of a high intellectual standard'. The minimum school leaving age was supposed to be 14, but exemptions were so easily obtained that 40 per cent of all school leavers in 1914 were below that age. Secondary schools obviously met resistance when they tried to establish a leaving age markedly higher than that for schools in general. And attempts to distinguish between secondary and higher elementary schools in terms of leaving age were on shaky ground. There were many secondary schools where the *maximum* leaving age was 15 or 16, and fewer than one in ten of all secondary school pupils in 1914 were older than 16. Such a struggle to maintain even a four-year course as normal in grammar schools meant that there was still no solid base from which sixth-form work could grow. Staying on was so often 'extraordinary'

6

that any marked increase in numbers had to wait until the conventional leaving age was nearer 16.

2. *Poor financial support*

Until 1907 secondary schools received no grants for pupils over the age of 16. Such pupils might exist, but they were not 'recognized' financially. Instead, grants were based on an assumed four-year course, the amount rising from £2 per pupil in the first year to £5 in the fourth. The new regulations for 1907 allowed £5 a year for each pupil aged 12-18, which meant a sharp increase in schools' resources. But no provision was made for the special expenses of advanced work, for the books, equipment and qualified teachers required. Nor were there maintenance allowances for those staying beyond the statutory leaving age, though these were repeatedly urged by the T.U.C. and the Labour Party. Local authorities *were* allowed by the Balfour Act to assist university students in cases of special need, but they did not do so on any large scale until the 1920s. The financial barriers to prolonged schooling were therefore considerable. Early wage earning must have seemed a duty to most able children from ordinary families, and the better opportunities and wages available to boys partly explain why girls at this time tended to stay longer at school.

3. *A 'chaos of examinations'*

The grammar school curriculum had broadened considerably since the mid-nineteenth century, when the teaching of classics was often 'an excuse for teaching nothing else'. It was tested by 'a plethora of different examinations . . . each with its own list of compulsory subjects and its own peculiarities of syllabus' (B.E., Annual

Report on Education, 1923-4, 26). The result was confusion, and a heavy strain on the schools.

In 1858 Oxford and Cambridge began their 'Local' examinations for those 'willing to accept the judgment of the universities on their general education'. A Higher Local was added in 1894 as a test of more advanced work. The Oxford and Cambridge Joint Board (1873) served those schools which sent large numbers to the 'ancient universities', and it at once offered a Higher Certificate as a sixth-form examination. London University's Matriculation examination, intended only as a qualification for its degree courses, came to be widely used as a rather superior leaving certificate. To prevent this misuse the university introduced an official leaving certificate to be taken at sixteen (1902), and a Higher Certificate (1905) for those who had already matriculated. Similar examinations were offered by Birmingham and, jointly, by the Northern universities. There were also university Intermediate examinations which could be taken at school, and which carried exemption from the preliminary part of a degree course.

Though many needs were met by this rapid growth, they were met haphazardly. Few universities accepted unconditionally the examinations of others, so that there were too many qualifications with a restricted currency. To add to the confusion, some professional organizations set their own examinations and made them compulsory; others accepted alternative evidence of ability, but laid down strict conditions for doing so. Civil Service examinations were a special case. Many 'crammers' existed solely to prepare candidates for them, and 17,000 secondary school pupils sat them in 1908 alone.

Schools therefore faced a variety of demands for special work quite impossible to meet when sixth forms were so small. Their senior pupils might be working for ten separate examinations, making class teaching impossible, and it was not unknown for headteachers to enter able pupils unnecessarily to boost their schools' record of successes. A widely canvassed remedy for this chaos was a system of school leaving certificates acceptable to all interested parties—individual employers, professional organizations and universities. This was officially recommended in 1911, and introduced six years later.

4. *The 'overlap' between schools and universities*

Gloomy comparisons with Germany were frequent in the education debates of 1902. And that inferiority so deplored at the secondary stage was apparent at the higher level. In 1911, there were 63,000 university students in Germany, and only 16,000 in Britain. Since supply so often creates demand in education, this scarcity of places seriously hampered advanced work in the schools.

A further problem was the competition between schools and universities for those aged 16-18. Matriculation was possible at 16, and entry to some universities could follow immediately. Evidence of sound general education was always demanded, but a Higher Certificate was often unnecessary. Specialization could either begin at school or after entry to a university, and many professors gave introductory courses, even in traditional school subjects, which assumed no previous knowledge. A British Association Committee which investigated this overlap in 1912 concluded that a good sixth form was usually far ahead of first-year university students, and that teaching of the 'elements' by universities was unavoidable. It did deplore, however, universities actually preparing students *for* matriculation.

The schools' case was clear. Universities were unnecessarily doing their job. Youngsters were being forced into studies for which they were not ready 'by the bribe of a degree at nineteen' when they could learn much more from active participation in the life of a school as responsible sixth formers. The Royal Commission on London University did recommend in 1913 that 17 should be the minimum age for entry, and that entry should depend not only on evidence of sound general education but on the successful completion at school of a more specialized course. 'The university should provide for the training of the adult, the school that of the adolescent.' This was precisely the schools' point. But it was some years yet before the battle was won.

5. A hierarchy of secondary schools

In the preface to the 1904 Regulations for Secondary Schools, it was stated that no secondary course could be considered complete which did not carry pupils to the age of 16; 'in schools of a high grade, which give an education leading on directly to the university, it *may* be continued up to the age of 18 or 19'. The definition was realistic, if unflattering. This classification of schools by leaving age and the presence or absence of a sixth form was commonplace at the time, and shows how precarious much advanced work was. The Board of Education's 'Memoranda' on secondary education (1913) has a comment on the size of many sixth forms which suggests a pained facing of the facts. 'One of the chief duties of secondary schools is to pass on to the universities a supply of pupils well prepared to begin degree work.' Yet the number of such pupils was often so small as to make class teaching impossible. It was better to be realistic. Schools with a low leaving age were advised to stick to 'first-rate work within clearly defined limits rather than attempt a more ambitious scheme in imitation of schools able to give a full course over eight or nine years'.

It is clear, then, that while the sixth form had 'associations of dignity and weight' in the public and large urban grammar schools, most grammar schools were still hampered by lack of numbers and resources, and bedevilled by a host of examinations. The very existence of a strong sixth form was a mark of superiority, as a flourishing G.C.E. course was later to be for a secondary modern school.

A 'New Deal' for the sixth form

1. A new examination system, 1917

In 1911 the Board of Education's Consultative Committee produced a detailed survey of external examinations in secondary schools. While acknowledging the good work of the various examining bodies, it deplored the 'multiplicity of examinations' which so interfered with the schools' work. A simple system of leaving certificates was to replace the variety of targets and qualifications. A first external examination was to be taken at the age of 16; this would 'test the attainments of an average pupil', and provide a 'guarantee of a good general education'. The high age limit was deliberately intended to persuade more grammar school pupils to stay on. A second examination at 18 was to test more intensive work in a few subjects. These School and Higher School Certificates would provide such evidence of fitness to enter employment, or professional training, or a university, as to make other external examinations unnecessary.

Official circulars were soon adding details to the plan. Teachers must have been relieved to learn that passes in School Certificate were to be within reach of 'pupils of reasonable industry and ordinary intelligence in an efficient secondary school'! Though the adjectives left room for interpretation, the intention was clear. A higher grade of pass, called a 'credit', was to serve as the matriculation standard for university entrants. The Higher Certificate was based on 'a more concentrated study of a connected group of subjects', with some subsidiary work from outside the group. No grant-aided school was to enter its pupils for any other external examination.

The examinations themselves, of course, were not new. It was the simplicity of the system which was to prove such an advantage to the schools. Delayed by the First World War, it was put into operation in 1917 under the supervision of the Secondary School Examinations Council (S.S.E.C.), a body representing teachers, examining boards, and local authorities. The Council's main duties were to maintain equal standards between the various boards, arrange conferences on common problems, and persuade universities and professional bodies to accept the two Certificates unconditionally in place of their own examinations. In this last task there were early successes to report. There were also complaints that there were only four teachers among the Council's seventeen members—poor representation, it was claimed, on a body with so much influence on the work of the schools.

2. *Special grants for advanced courses, 1917*

In April 1917 H. A. L. Fisher's maiden speech as President of the Board of Education included the announcement of special grants for sixth-form courses 'so planned as to lead up to a standard required for entering upon an honours course at a university'. Grants of £400 per course would pay the salary of a suitably qualified teacher, with

12

something over for books and equipment; graduate salaries then ranged from £240-£500 for men, and £225-£400 for women. The grants were not startingly generous, but sixth-form work had received no special help before.

Strict conditions were soon laid down as to what courses were acceptable. Though specialization was assumed, there was also something of that insistence on integration and breadth found in recent debates on the sixth-form curriculum. A recognized Advanced Course had to offer 'continuous and systematic instruction in a group of subjects which have organic unity'. Three such groups were suggested—Classical Studies, Mathematics and Science, and Modern Studies, i.e. History, French and Latin (the original inclusion of German as the third modern subject was for the moment emotionally impossible). All schools with a sixth form were to aim at providing one of these courses. Few could provide all three, especially since each had to be taken by a 'sufficient number' to make class teaching possible. Schools were therefore to co-operate in a mutual exchange of pupils so that each course could be provided somewhere accessible to any prospective student. Bearing in mind the perennial complaint that sixth-form work is too academic for those not concerned with university entry, it is interesting that the three courses were described as suitable only for those intending to take honours degrees; those not bound for university at all needed quite different provision (B.E. Circular 1023, 1917).

The precarious nature of so much sixth-form work before 1917 brought a warm welcome for the new grants. It was hoped that they would 'secure a regular flow of the most competent to the universities and other places of higher humanistic and technical education', and bring many schools 'for the first time into the full current of university life' (*T.E.S.*, 3 May 1917). But there were also fears and complaints reminiscent of more recent arguments over sixth-form colleges and the 'viability' of sixth-form work in small selective, and in most unselective, schools. For large schools with advanced work already well established, prospects of getting one or more of these special grants were good. For the ordinary grammar school, aid might still be out of reach; it might then be branded as inferior, lose its ablest pupils, and decline still further. In a letter to Fisher, the Headmasters' Association recognized the 'stimulus to advanced work provided in a limited number of schools' but expressed alarm at the prospect of a still clearer distinction between these few and the rest. In his reply, Fisher denied any intention of forcing schools which failed to get grants to give up all advanced teaching; indeed, he expected a rapid rise in the number able to provide it. But 'concentration of provision *is* called for, especially by the inadequate supply of teachers with high qualifications'. The teachers were unconvinced, an I.A.A.M. policy statement in 1922 urging that 'every secondary school should be so equipped as to provide to the age of 18 in all branches of the curriculum'.

On one side were the obvious arguments for rationalization, for the economic use of staff and equipment. Fisher described as the sensible target, not all courses in every school, but all courses in each 'area of accessibility'. This obviously meant the frequent transfer of pupils. There was even talk of a 'secondary university', concentrating on advanced work and so able to offer a full range of subjects. This was less prophetic than it might seem, for large grammar schools had long accepted entrants at 16 from neighbours unable to cope with sixth-form demands. Against such arguments were the fervent objections of headteachers at losing their oldest and ablest pupils. The rest of the school would be denied sixth-form leadership

14

and influence, morale and status would suffer, able staff would leave, and pupils themselves would be unsettled by a change of school at the crucial age of 15 or 16.

There were also criticisms of the way some schools met the Board's requirements—of pupils being 'press-ganged' into advanced courses to drum up the necessary numbers, of main subjects being given undue prominence in the main school to guarantee recruits, of headteachers so anxious to earn the grants that children were entering the sixth form at 14 and being 'over-pressed'. Behind most of this criticism was the feeling that the Board's conditions were too strict. Though new courses were introduced, and other main subjects accepted, e.g. English and Geography, the number of schools earning grants did not rise after 1922, when it represented one-third of boys' grammar schools and one-fifth of those for girls. The grants had given an initial impetus to advanced work in many schools, and had influenced many others which were not officially recognized as deserving them; but the whole distinction between 'advanced courses' and other sixth-form work was felt to be unreal. All work of post-matriculation standard, and any combination of subjects, deserved financial support. In 1933 the Board accepted the full force of 'tendencies towards experiment, freedom and individuality' (B.E. Circular 1441, 1935). Additional grants were now to be given for each pupil under the age of 19 at the start of the school year who was following a course beyond School Certificate level; they were on a sliding scale to help small schools—£16 for each of the first 15 pupils, £12 for the next 15, £10 for all others. Hundreds of schools benefited for the first time from the new system which provided a strong financial inducement for expanding their sixth forms.

2

Slow growth, 1920-1944

In 1920 the future playwright Emlyn Williams joined six other pupils in the 'Honours Form' of Holyhead County School. All took History, French and English—though with only three teachers, 'women with the rest of the school on their hands', most of their lessons were unsupervised. It was his good fortune that one of the three had a personality 'which demanded a university platform facing a gallery'. She fed his devouring interest in literature, gave him books, passed on her weekly copy of the *Observer*, planned his long visit to France, and paid the entrance fee for the Oxford scholarship which he won (Williams, 1961). The historian A. L. Rowse was then at a Cornish secondary school. Its headmaster reinforced his determination to get to Oxford, but it was Rowse who did the work. No regular teaching was provided for the sixth form, and one able master left suddenly. 'If I had not been used to working on my own, doing my own reading and, so far as I could, directing my own course, it might have been disastrous.' His scholarship to the same college as Emlyn Williams was greeted at school with great jubilation—'tennis all the afternoon, icecream and tea at four o'clock and, I think, a whole holiday' (Rowse, 1942).

Both boys came from poor homes and small schools.

Both were successful against very heavy odds. Many like them, able but less brilliant or less fortunate, had little chance of higher education. How much progress was there in the next twenty years towards those aims set out in 1917—'to prolong the school life of many able pupils, provide increased facilities for more thorough work in higher forms of reasonable size . . . and distribute university scholarships among a wider class'?

Sixth-form numbers

The reforms of 1917 were soon followed by bursts of official optimism about their effects. Many schools were doing advanced work of a kind previously restricted to a few, and this was 'the most striking evidence of progress, not merely in the extent but in the quality of secondary education' (B.E., 1923-4, 27). Far more schools could claim a sixth-form as 'the flower of their work and social life', and recall complacently the 'pitiable expedients' once needed to keep it alive. The total number of sixth formers in grammar schools certainly rose steeply—from under 10,000 in 1912 to 20,000 in 1926, and to almost 40,000 in 1937. But this was largely because of the general expansion in secondary education. Sixth-forms were larger because secondary schools were larger, and there was no steady 'trend' towards longer school life such as appeared in the 1950s.

Age distribution in grammar schools (March 31 of each year)

	Under 16	16-17	17-18	18-19
	%	%	%	%
1920	87	8	4	1
1926	83	10	5	2
1932	82	10	5	3
1938	84	10	4	2
(1966, January)	75	12	9	4

17

The proportion staying on into the sixth form rose during the late 1920s. It reached an 'artificially' high level among boys during the worst years of the Depression, bringing anxious discussion of how best to cater for those who simply drifted into the sixth form until employment prospects improved. The peak was reached in 1932. Girls were less affected, partly because clerical work and those professions open to them were less vulnerable in the slump, partly because many parents still valued grammar schools for their daughters more as finishing schools than as the means to a career. In the late 1930s there was a sharp drop in the proportion of boys and girls staying on, a trend noted with concern in the Spens Report. Numbers entering grammar schools were unusually high in 1931-32 because of the post-war bulge in the birth rate, and schools may have found difficulty in coping with the larger intake. Whatever the reasons for the drop, there was certainly no cause at the end of this period to expect any massive increase in sixth-form numbers.

Sixth formers remained, in most schools, a select minority—an elite naturally entrusted with school duties and rewarded with privileges. In 1938, 40 per cent of grammar schools had fewer than 300 pupils. Their sixth forms can rarely have exceeded twenty, and some faced 'demotion' to secondary modern status in 1944 because their advanced work was so slight. Large schools, especially in suburban areas and especially in London and the South-east, tended to keep a higher proportion of their pupils. But few were large enough, except in the most favourable circumstances, to provide a wide range of sixth-form courses. In the bitter arguments over comprehensive education after 1944, the bogey of size was often raised. Schools would become too large, because even a 4-5 stream entry, if unselected, might provide only eight or nine sixth formers a year. It was then pointed out that this had been a normal and acceptable figure before the War 'in the average grammar school' (*T.E.S.*, 12 March 1949, 179).

It was still tempting, then, to argue that grammar schools should be so 'graded' as to concentrate advanced work in those best able to provide it. The argument was firmly rejected in the Spens Report. All should provide 'preparation for a university in at least *one* subject', as a stimulus to the rest of the school. But attempts to do more than this were often wildly wasteful of staff—as at one school where 'twenty-three children were receiving the equivalent of the full-time attention of three teachers . . . the tuition being sometimes individual'. To avoid waste and duplication the mutual transfer of sixth formers was obviously desirable (Spens, 1938, 333-7). The continued inadequacy of much sixth-form work is also reflected in the Report's objections to multilateral schools. 'There is general agreement that much of what is most valuable in the grammar school tradition depends upon the existence of a sixth form. But a sixth form can only play its traditional part in the life of a school if it contains a reasonably high proportion of its pupils.' This was difficult to secure even in selected schools, because of 'the large proportion of pupils who leave before or about the age of sixteen' (Spens, 1938, xx).

Factors affecting sixth-form development

1. *Early Leaving*

Secondary schools were officially described in 1904 as offering a general education 'up to and beyond the age of 16'. This flattered many of them, those which found difficulty in maintaining even a four-year course. It became a more realistic description in the 1920s, largely through the free place system. More free places meant more able pupils, a survey in London in 1933 showing only half the fee-payers and almost all the free-placers as being of 'high ability' (Gray & Moshinsky, 1938, 357). The fierce competition for places helped local authorities to standardize the age of entry at 11-12, and obtain guarantees from parents that those selected would stay a 'full course'. Often more committed to the school, they tended to stay longer anyway. In 1926, for example, the average secondary school life of fee-payers was 3 years and 5 months; of those with free places, it was 4 years and 3 months.

Plans to raise the school-leaving age were swallowed up by the economic crisis of 1931, and by the outbreak of war on the very day 'appointed' for it in 1939. And though growing numbers were staying on voluntarily, even in the elementary schools, the gap between the statutory minimum and the leaving age demanded by a full secondary course remained wide enough to face many parents with hard decisions and heavy sacrifices. Whether these seemed worthwhile depended on the prospect of future rewards. The proportion of 'tertiary' occupations in the total labour force—e.g. those in banking, administration and the professions—was certainly rising, and entry to them depended increasingly on written qualifications. Employers' willingness to see a School Certificate as clear evidence of all-round ability gave it an obvious vocational value. Their even higher regard for 'Matriculation'—those 'credits' demanded by universities as entrance qualifications —was often attacked as distorting the schools' work by forcing too many to a standard intended only for the few. These were strong inducements to stay on until 16, especially when the Depression emphasized the relative security of 'white-collar' employment, and openings dwindled in many industries. Labour leaders, indeed, some-times asked for the leaving age to be raised so as to keep some 450,000 young workers a year from the competition for jobs.

But the effects of the Depression were not all one way. Many stayed at school hoping for things to improve, and when the improvement came in the late 1930s, the propor-tion entering the sixth form fell sharply. Many others must have forfeited their ambitions and played safe for modest jobs. 'Secondary education was prized as a qualification for the more clerical of such jobs, but the aspirant to them must generally leave at 16, for the longer he stayed, the nearer he approached the dangerous age for employment, which was tending to shift upwards' (Percy, 1941, 112). The worst years of mass unemployment also forced economy campaigns on local authorities. Maintenance allowances were restricted, either by cutting their value or by raising the minimum level of parental income below which they were paid. At the same time unemployment, or the risk of it, left many parents unable to support pro-longed schooling even if places were free.

Such generalizations conceal marked regional differences. A national figure of 10 per cent unemployed had risen to 24 per cent by 1932. It then fell to just under 12 per cent in 1937. In 1935, the unemployment rate in London and the South-east was only 6 per cent, compared with 14 per cent in the North and 22 per cent in Wales (Mowat, 1955, 464). Real income per capita of the *occupied* population increased about 20 per cent during the inter-War period, bringing sharp contrasts between the 'depressed areas' and the comparatively prosperous South-east and Midlands. The proportion staying on at school therefore varied widely according to poverty and employment prospects in the immediate area. In 1925, boys over 16 represented 26 per cent of those aged 11-16 in London secondary schools, 22 per cent in Coventry, 17 per cent in Bristol, 11 per cent in Bradford, and 8 per cent in Halifax. Unfortunately, the Board of Education then stopped publishing such detailed figures, but differences must have been far greater at the height of the Depression, when its statistics show only the high proportion of older pupils in London, where there was so much 'white-collar' employment.

One generalization can be made. Half the secondary-school leavers of 1920 were under 16. This had fallen to one-third by 1926. But it was no lower in 1938, when rather more than one-third left without sitting the School Certificate examination. Even this was a great improvement on the situation before 1914. But when so many left early, there was obviously no 'natural passage' into the sixth form. Advanced work in schools was still restricted by the narrow base from which it grew.

2. *The sixth form and careers*

It is often assumed, quite wrongly, that most sixth formers thirty or forty years ago were bound for some university or college, and that academic work was their natural diet. Certainly, general courses—common enough in girls' schools—were miserably lacking for boys. Yet, in 1937, half the candidates in Higher Certificate examinations were not intending to continue their full-time education (S.S.E.C., 1939, 5). What could staying on offer those who would begin work at 17 or 18? What was Higher Certificate worth as a qualification?

A School Certificate, highly regarded by employers and an indispensable first step to higher education, was an obvious prize of a successful secondary school course. The Higher Certificate lacked such clear-cut advantages. In the early 1920s it was still not essential for matriculation, and universities continued to provide introductory courses and Intermediate examinations for those who had not yet specialized. But this was a battle the schools were winning. The number of 'premature students' dwindled away as 'Higher' became an unavoidable test of fitness for university study. Progress was also made in persuading professional organizations to accept passes at that level in place of their own entrance examinations. But teachers still doubted whether industry and commerce were really interested in their older pupils. When the Headmasters' Association set up its own Employment Committee in 1922, one of its main aims was to persuade employers that there were two distinct leaving ages from grammar schools—at 16 and at 18—and that it was the ablest who stayed on. But efforts to win advantages in pay or seniority for the older recruit had little success. The benefits of prolonged schooling were not always apparent, and employers tended to argue—'If his qualities are what you say, they will soon make themselves felt without any need for special privileges'.

Industrialists seemed especially unhelpful, as though they were conditioned to take people either at 14 or at graduate level. A headmasters' conference in 1924 was told by the chairman of Metropolitan Vickers that engineering took three broad classes of recruit—up to 16 for skilled trades, at 18 for 'first and second lieutenants', and graduates for key posts. Since he added that the demand for graduates was ten times that for 'lieutenants', his analogy was a poor one—lieutenants are the most numerous of army officers, and are fairly rapidly promoted, while the 18-year old industrial recruit had only faint prospects of high managerial rank. In fact, engineering firms remained reluctant to accept older boys for apprenticeships, partly

23

because of trades union opposition to any real concessions to them, partly because of the risk of restlessness and frustration long before the end of training. The Head-masters' Employment Committee therefore warned schools to accept 16 as the latest age for entry to this industry unless a degree course was intended.

Grammar schools were often blamed at this time for diverting too many of their ablest pupils from industry to commerce and the professions by their 'narrowly academic' outlook (Banks, 1955, 168-97). Yet when industrialists addressed meetings of teachers, they rarely called for more science, or economics, or technical drawing. The emphasis was usually on those qualities of leadership and sportsman-ship supposedly developed in the grammar schools, and on the virtues of 'humane learning'. There was also a natural bias towards white-collar occupations which had little to do with the schools. These occupations offered 'better financial rewards, quicker and more certain promotion, easier hours and conditions of work, greater security'. They also offered 'a more obvious recognition of the higher educational standard of the recruit' (H.R., March 1932, 54). This last point was especially true of the professions, where a Higher Certificate sometimes allowed the holder to by-pass preliminary examinations and enter some way above the bottom rung. Recruitment and training in commerce were more haphazard, and the best that the Committee on Education for Salesmanship could say in 1931 was that while 18 was not always too late for entry, there were few advantages in coming in so late. But there were clear signs in the 1930s that those leaving with Higher Certificates were becoming easier to place. There were more openings in the Civil Service, local government, the armed forces, banks and insurance companies, and the administrative side of some industries.

In girls' schools, the impact of employment prospects was somewhat less marked because parents were often more interested in the social and cultural benefits of a sixth-form course than in its direct vocational value. Of course, the number of 'higher' occupations open to women was increasing. When Miss Buss, the famous headmistress and pioneer of girls' secondary education, sent written evidence to the Bryce Commission (1895), she described 'first-grade' schools for girls as those where leavers 'either go home or proceed to places of higher education'; from 'second-grade' schools, 'they either go home, or go out into the Civil Service or similar employment'. The choice was wider in the 1930s. The main outlets for older girls were teaching, nursing and other medical auxiliary services, and the less routine kinds of secretarial work. Teaching was especially attractive, and twice as many women entered Training Colleges as went on to universities. Though Higher Certificate passes were not usually required by the Colleges, one year's preparation in a sixth form was common and two was sometimes recommended.

A sixth-form course was certainly not the sure passport to success that it later seemed to be. It was still not possible for headteachers to be blandly confident of their case when asked by parents—'What can you promise if I leave him at school till eighteen?' There were still strong pressures to regard 16 as the 'normal' leaving age for those not clearly bound for a university or college.

3. Growth in higher education

The foundation statutes of many ancient grammar schools show them as 'primarily designed to prepare scholars to proceed to the universities . . . [they were] from one point of view vocational schools directed towards the universities' (Spens, 1938, 6). If this was ever more than theory, it was certainly not so in the early years of this century. In 1910, over a half the grant-aided grammar schools sent no pupils at all to a university. One in three failed to do so in 1924, and one in seven had sent none over a whole five-year period (B.E. Statistics, 1926, 66). But the number without a regular 'university connection' was falling rapidly. Even so, the provision of university places lagged far behind the expansion in secondary education. The number of students in British universities rose from 20,000 in 1920 to 42,000 in 1924, and to 50,000 in 1938—an increase of 150 per cent in almost forty years. The same period brought a 500 per cent increase in secondary school places. The University Grants Committee itself made some unflattering international comparisons. In 1934, the total number of inhabitants for every university student was 125 in the United States, 473 in Scotland, 480 in France, 604 in Germany, 808 in Italy, and 1,013 in England. The Committee went on to refer to fears, common at the time, of unemployment among graduates and an 'overproduction of intellectuals'. But it did not look as though 'there is an unduly liberal provision of university facilities here, unless it be held that it is being altogether overdone elsewhere' (U.G.C. 1934-5, 28). That 'unless' was highly unconvincing. Higher education was still assumed to be for the few, and this assumption, together with the financial burdens involved, did much to check sixth-form growth. So far were the grammar schools from being 'preparatory schools for the universities', that the proportion of leavers going there actually declined between 1932 and 1937—from 7 per cent to 5 per cent of the boys, and 4 per cent to 3 per cent of the girls. The proportion going to Training Colleges also fell, partly perhaps because a declining birthrate—it reached its lowest point in 1933—brought prophecies of a sharp *and continuing* drop in the school population. When all forms of further education are taken into account, 87 per cent boys leaving secondary schools in 1936-7, and 73 per cent girls, ended their formal education at that point (Spens, 1938, 102).

4. *Grants and scholarships*

Though university places were in short supply, there was no hectic scramble for them. Finance provided a rigorous means of selection, and the real competition was for the means to support a course of higher education. Even in 1938 only 40 per cent of university students were receiving any help from public funds. A survey a few years later found the number of scholarships sufficient for the really brilliant, but quite inadequate for the far greater number of able students who were capable of sound university work (British Association for the Advancement of Science, 1944, 6).

Some schools provided university scholarships out of their own funds, the result of wills and endowments often centuries old. Such scholarships were limited in scope and most unevenly distributed. So were those offered by universities. Dominating them in number, value and prestige were those awarded by the colleges of Oxford and Cambridge. But they were beyond the reach of most grammar school pupils; in 1935, for example, 75 per cent were won by candidates from public schools. Scholarships elsewhere were scarce, though Liverpool and Sheffield, for example, were relatively generous because of endowments from local industries.

The government made its first direct grants to university students in 1920. These 'state scholarships' were initially restricted to pupils from grant-aided schools so as to—

'strengthen the weak links between them and the universities'. They were awarded for outstanding results in Higher Certificate examinations, and the maximum amount of £80 per annum was very generous by local authority standards. The first offering was 200, raised to 300 in 1930 and to 360 in 1936. Even that last number was only 10 per cent of the annual university intake from grammar schools. But the scholarships set the pace for local authority awards; they meant status as well as money, and were especially valuable to girls because the total scholarship provision for them was so meagre. By 1936 there were fifteen candidates for each state scholarship awarded. The degree results of their holders were proudly published in Board of Education reports, and there were complaints that they were 'impoverishing the modern universities' because an increasing proportion—36 per cent in 1921, 70 per cent in 1937—were taking them up at Oxford or Cambridge. The post-war Labour government was to try a short-lived 'quota system' to bring a fairer distribution of talent.

The Balfour Act had cautiously *permitted* local education authorities to 'assist' university students. After a slow start, the number so assisted grew rapidly. In 1935-6, 4,847 men and 1,704 women were receiving university grants from their local authorities; a further 741 men and 1,854 women were being helped through Training College courses. Even so, these awards were more often seen as prizes for the outstanding rather than as logical extensions of the free place system. Their value was usually well below official estimates of the cost of residence and tuition at the various universities. And there were unjustly wide differences between local authorities in the number given, their amount, the scale for parental contributions, and the method of selection. In 1930, only eighteen made awards comparable to state scholarships—i.e. up to £80. Some made £50 their top limit, some seemed to think £20 was generous, and some refused to name a sum until other forms of assistance had been disclosed, so that students from poor homes usually needed not one but a 'hand' of scholarships. A. L. Rowse provides a good example of this. The national economy drive of 1922 left his county of Cornwall with only two 'miserable' scholarships of £60 per annum. 'It was very worrying; I had to be sure of one of them, and even then £60 was a very little way to the £200 I would need to go to Oxford.' Since state scholarships were a temporary casualty of this economy drive, he went for and won an Oxford scholarship worth £80. He was then interviewed by one of those City of London companies which made awards of their own, asked how much he thought necessary to go to Oxford, and given the extra money (Rowse, 1942, 250 & 266-9).

Many local authority scholarships were conditional on the student's promise to enter teaching. There were similar awards for those who stayed on in secondary schools over the age of sixteen. Nearly 5,000 were given in 1922, but the number fell sharply after fierce attacks on them as 'bribes' and as a thoroughly unworthy means of recruitment. There were also Intermediate awards, with no strings attached, for those 'doing advanced work in secondary schools'. Many of them meant no more than the payment of fees, but in 1935-6 for example, 8,335 sixth formers were receiving their fees and small maintenance allowances—the average value of these being £14 per annum.

In theory, the principle was slowly being accepted that none should be debarred by lack of money from opportunities he deserved. In practice, progress was slow. Many could still consider a prolonged education only at heavy cost to their parents, and so were often forced by circumstances to abandon the idea.

Social selection in secondary education

'Secondary education for all', meant an end to 'selection by
elimination'. All were to go forward, 'though along different paths'. There had therefore to be parity of esteem
between secondary schools of different types (Hadow,
1926, 71). Logically correct, this proved practically impossible. Even the *term* 'secondary' was reserved for the
grammar schools. Their unique position was firmly founded
on tradition, a highly selected intake, the prestige of a
'liberal education' reinforced by employers' enthusiasm for
School Certificate, and the rewards of the occupations for
which they prepared. They produced, said H. A. L. Fisher,
strangely forgetting the public schools, 'all the leaders, the
leaders in commerce and industry, in politics and law, the
leaders in the church, the leaders in the state' (*A.M.A.*,
February 1920, 8). They offered entry to higher education
for the few, the relative security of white collar employment for the many. It is not surprising that equality of
opportunity was so often interpreted as widening the
'ladder' to the grammar schools rather than as developing
alternatives to them.

Certainly the ladder was widened. In 1918, 30 per cent
of the pupils in grant-aided secondary schools held free
places. In 1937, 44 per cent were paying nothing at all
and 7 per cent only part fees; many schools took only those
successful in open scholarship examinations. But in the
fierce competition for places it was not always the ablest
who were chosen. Many free places were rejected by
parents unable to support a long schooling, especially when
maintenance allowances were cut back in the early 1930s.
Some able children from poor homes were not entered at
all, hence demands that the scholarship examination be

made compulsory. Though group intelligence tests were increasingly used in 'borderline' cases, written tests of English and arithmetic remained the standard procedure. For all these reasons, the odds were heavily weighted against children from working-class homes. From a survey in London in 1933 it was estimated that 'on the highest criterion of ability 45 per cent, and on the lowest 59 per cent, of the total number of gifted children in the school population do not enjoy the opportunity of a (secondary) education' (Gray & Moshinsky, 1938, 367).

The difference in 'life chances', so glaring at the point of entry to grammar schools, widened still further within them. This process of social selection, so clearly documented for a later period in the Crowther and other reports, was an even more ruthless sifting of the fortunate from the unfortunate when the financial burdens of prolonged schooling were less certainly offset by the prospect of future rewards, and when higher education often depended on scarce and inadequate scholarships. Even in the late 1930s working-class children could hardly 'drift' into the sixth form. Entry was unusual enough to need clear evidence of academic ability and uncommon ambition in the parents. It was 'professional and middle-class parents' who might see 18 as the age when 'their own children, almost irrespective of ability, should leave school and go out into the world' (Crowther, 1959, 62). Of those born 1910-29, an estimated 39 per cent of boys with fathers in non-manual occupations had some form of secondary education, compared with only 10 per cent from working-class homes; the figures for girls were 36 per cent and 9 per cent. Class differences in chances of going to a university were obviously greater still—8.5 per cent compared with 1.4 per cent for boys and 4 per cent compared with 0.2 per cent for girls (Floud, 1954).

Sixth formers, then, were not necessarily the intellectual elite of their age group. But they were very much a social elite, temptingly easy to train for leadership of a traditional kind. Their 'general culture' was often taken for granted, so reducing anxiety about general studies and the need to 'make up for' the home. The real challenge to their customary place in the school, and to the customary emphasis on specialized study, was to come from that 'explosion' in sixth-form numbers which began in the 1950s.

3

The Sixth-form curriculum, 1917-1944

There was a consensus of opinion about the nature and scope of sixth-form work. Some degree of specialization was essential. This had to be supplemented by more general studies. The Higher Certificate was a valuable servant, but a dangerous master because it imposed on many an unsuitably heavy burden of academic work. This was especially true of those sixth formers not going on to some form of higher education; they needed separate provision.

Such ideas were distorted, even contradicted, in practice. Wide agreement about what sixth-form work ought to be is matched by a concentration of criticism on certain crucial weaknesses. There seemed to be too much specialization, hopes of a balanced curriculum were being borne down by rising standards in main courses, and sixth formers with all their various needs were being pushed into the single mould of academic study.

Theory and practice

1. Specialization

The most obvious characteristic of sixth-form work, marking it off from the 'sound general education' of the main school, was the study of a few subjects in depth. It was the declared purpose of the Higher Certificate to test 'a more concentrated study of a connected group of subjects', and of the Advanced Course grants to support work suitable as preparation for an honours degree which occupied a 'predominant part' of the pupil's time.

Teacher opinion seemed to accept the value of specialization. It stimulated interest, maintained high standards of work, kept teachers close to university methods and material and added to their status. A speaker at one conference of grammar school masters met complaints of over-specialization with the fervent plea—'Please let no one take away the undergraduate work from the top of the secondary schools. It has been the making of them, it is the charm of the whole business' (A.M.A., January 1934, 38).

The most common defence of specialization was its contribution to the intellectual development of the sixth former. It was a discipline in itself, a 'true' introduction to learning. A foreign observer might well have asked why such virtues were less obvious elsewhere. A wide range of subjects, continued throughout a secondary-school course, was the normal pattern in e.g. Scotland, France, Germany and the United States. Nowhere else was highly specialized work begun so early. It was indeed the 'English system of study in depth' (Crowther, 1959, 259). This uniqueness has been explained by the relative absence of state control over the curriculum. During the nineteenth century, new subjects clamoured for a place in the time-table. Were they to be included in a 'balanced' course, or made alternatives to the traditional 'liberal studies'? In France and Germany, for example, governments insisted on the first solution. In England, schools were left more to their own devices. This meant, not freedom of choice, but subjection to what might be called market pressures—the high prestige of 'liberal studies' even in the eyes of employers, the overweighting of university scholarships on that side, the danger of wasting teachers on too wide a front when advanced work was so limited in many schools (Peterson, 1960, 8-10). The great public schools were perhaps at the height of their prestige when the Balfour Act was passed. Their curriculum was still narrow, with the emphasis heavily on 'humane learning', and it was obviously tempting for the new and revived grammar schools to follow an established pattern. Nor was there that awareness of the importance of mathematics and science to an industrial society which made those subjects compulsory throughout a secondary school in other countries.

The most serious doubts here about intensive specialization came from women teachers. They dealt with a far smaller proportion of university entrants, and Training Colleges were more general in their demands. They also had to provide many one-year courses for those entering nursing or commerce. They were therefore active in demanding a separate examination for non-specialists, with perhaps five subjects at a level somewhere between Higher and School Certificate. A long battle was fought over this. But the relevant point here is that such proposals, which could have been firmly supported by the example of other countries, were rejected as an unjustifiable watering-down of academic standards, and a threat to the whole foundation of sixth-form work. Even so, they represented an alternative to specialization, not a general rejection of it.

What was the 'unit of specialization' to be—a number of 'sovereign subjects', or an integrated course? All the emphasis in the 1917 grant regulations had been on the second, on 'continuous, coherent and systematic instruction in a group of subjects which have organic unity' Three main courses were recognized initially—in Science and

Mathematics, Classical Studies, and Modern Studies—and any recognized course had to include enough subsidiary work to 'support' and 'balance' the specialized work. This belief in 'coherence' resembles recent curriculum reform in universities, with their combined courses in, for example, European Studies. Many schools, indeed, had their applications for Advanced Course grants rejected because they were offering what the Board ponderously called 'an arbitrarily selected collection of disparate subjects' (B.E. Circular 1112, 1919). Though they were soon relaxed under pressure from the schools, the regulations were still attacked as restrictive, as an attempt at official control over the curriculum, and there was general relief when they were replaced in 1935 by a system of per capita grants for sixth formers (see chapter 1).

The same demand for an unrestricted choice of subjects is found in the two external examinations. School Certificate candidates had to obtain passes in each of three groups. This was an attempt to guarantee a broad course. Art, music, woodwork and other such 'extras' were placed in a fourth and optional group, the low status of which was felt to symbolize the over-academic curriculum of the grammar school. Higher Certificate, testing a specialized course, required passes from only one group of subjects. Though there was strong encouragement to look outside it for subsidiary work, this was felt as a barrier to combined courses in Arts and Science. And while the group system had been modified almost out of existence by 1939, the schools could hardly benefit as long as universities continued to lay down precisely what they demanded of their entrants.

Subjects in Higher Certificate could be taken at principal or subsidiary level, and—as in recent Schools Council proposals—various combinations of the two were possible.

36

It was the great hope of those concerned with over-specialization that the various needs of the sixth form could be met within this framework. Most examining boards based their Certificates on two or more main subjects; fewer than two would dilute the essential ingredient of study in depth. Unfortunately, fewer than *three* main passes were regarded suspiciously by universities and local authorities. This was a powerful reason for specialization and for the crowding out of general work. The role of the subsidiary subject was hard to define. Sometimes it 'supported' the main subject, as English might support history or mathematics support physics. Sometimes it was introduced as 'contrast'. But at what level of difficulty? There were references to 'a sound working knowledge', and 'half a main subject' was a common formula. Certainly, its uses were varied. Despite official disapproval, subsidiaries were sometimes used as a trial run for the main examination. They provided some evidence of attainment for those leaving the sixth form after one year. And they were a way of broadening advanced work, offering an objective to those taking up extra subjects or continuing ones done in School Certificate in a less fact-grinding way.

The table of Higher Certificate entries shows the decline of Latin and Greek, the rise of geography to academic respectability, some decline in the proportion taking science, and a widening range of subjects being offered.

Subject	1920		1938	
	No. of entries	% total	No. of entries	% total
Latin & Greek	1,196	17	3,470	9
French	996	15	4,752	13
German	90	1·5	899	2
Spanish			138	
English	573	8	4,734	13
History	472	7	3,880	10
Geography	100	1·5	1,795	5
Economics			179	

Mathematics	1,289	19	5,501	15
Physics	1,006	15	4,040	11
Chemistry	1,016	15	3,934	11
Biol. & Zoology	26		1,558	4
Art & Music			252	

2. *Specialization to excess*

The proper scope of sixth-form work had been carefully defined by the Board of Education in 1913. It was not to anticipate what was done in the universities, 'either in methods of study or in the nature of the curriculum'. It was to provide, not detailed knowledge, but 'that preliminary knowledge essential to a specialized study' (B.E. Memoranda, 1913, 20). This was a sensible warning against doing too much. But in practice standards were steadily driven upwards, partly by university requirements, mainly by the competition for scholarships. The proportion of passes was generally less in the Higher than in the School Certificate, and a bare pass, of course, was no use for those hoping for a state scholarship or a major local authority award. There were complaints too that it was not only the burden of factual knowledge that was heavy. In Arts subjects especially, where opinions and judgments were asked for, the pupil was said to be forced into insincerity because he lacked the mental, emotional or practical experience to answer honestly and had to be taught sophisticated responses.

The claims of general education were easily forgotten under this heavy pressure, and the universities themselves often criticised the narrow outlook of their entrants. Yet there was agreement in theory that not more than two-thirds, or at most three-quarters, of the sixth-form time-table was to be devoted to specialized work. How was this to be supplemented? Objectives were often strikingly ambitious—e.g. that sixth formers should leave school 'well versed in all the main tendencies of modern life'—and often numbingly vague—e.g. that they should acquire 'a sort of background of what you might call general cultural subjects' (*A.M.A.*, February 1931, 6; *H.R.*, March 1931, 19). But though there were few explicit prophecies of the later 'Two Cultures' debate, there was a general belief in a balanced curriculum. Compulsory papers in art or philosophy or current affairs were often called for to 'guarantee some broadening of the mind', and subsidiary subjects provided an obvious way of including work quite different from the main course. Then as now, however, there was far less concern for 'broadening' Arts students, who surely needed the same balance of science that many schools gave to their scientists in languages or modern history. And since the pressure to take three main subjects at Higher Certificate was strong, and these had to be taken normally from the same group, there was a built-in bias towards heavy specialization which was difficult to resist.

3. *General courses*

Belief in the value of specialization was always qualified by this demand for adequate supplementary work. It was qualified most strongly by concern for those not intending to continue their formal education beyond the sixth form. Did they need a specialized course at all?

The advanced course grants of 1917 had been designed to encourage 'university-directed work'. It was pointed out that many sixth formers would fare better by carrying on a more general education (B.E. Circular 1112, 1919). The Higher Certificate, however, was supposed to serve two purposes, providing both a means of entry to higher education, and a higher leaving certificate, 'a suitable test of two years work for the average pupil'. If it became too narrowly academic and specialized it could obviously not perform this second function. That it *had* become so, for reasons which will be considered later in the chapter, was a perennial complaint from the schools.

One possible remedy was to juggle with the balance between principal and subsidiary subjects, to allow the less academic to take three or even four of their five subjects at the subsidiary level. A more radical suggestion was for a separate examination altogether. In 1926 the Secondary School Examinations Council referred in its report to 'some lowering in the average quality of candidates' as sixth-form numbers rose, and to consequent demands for a 'less ambitious course of study' (B.E., 1927, 29). Two years later it proposed a new Intermediate Certificate, at a standard somewhere between the School and Higher Certificates. There were some favourable reactions, especially from girls' schools, but predictable protests that some intensive study was essential in any true sixth-form course. It was also argued that a new examination would send standards at the existing level even higher, and put new burdens on schools already hard pushed to provide adequate advanced teaching. The proposal got nowhere. Years later the Norwood Committee was still tackling this problem of an examination with the 'two irreconcilable functions' of providing a qualification for higher education, and a superior leaving certificate. Its solution was to separate the two, introducing a special examination for those competing for university scholarships and so freeing Higher Certificate for its 'proper' purpose of providing evidence that a sixth-form course had been satisfactorily completed (Norwood, 1943, 41).

This was a solution within the framework of an academic examination. It would reduce the pressure on many sixth

40

formers, but they would still be taking an academic course. What of those who would leave the sixth form for employment at 17 or 18, and who were not capable of, or not interested in, academic study? This is a problem which *has* to be faced in the expanded sixth forms of the 1960s. It was touched on briefly in the Spens Report thirty years ago. Such pupils were 'a new and important element in the sixth form', to be actively encouraged by special courses and perhaps some preliminary vocational training (Spens, 1938, 166). Such courses were common in girls' schools, where many pupils wanted a year's general work before entering teaching, nursing or commerce, and the Assistant Mistresses' Association published in 1939 a survey of *Sixth Form Life and Work* which concentrated on those who 'are unwilling to specialize and prefer a less intensive course of study'. Such girls needed a goal which 'released them from examination requirements altogether', and examples were given of commercial courses—shorthand and typing with a wide range of general work—of 'cultural' courses based on art and literature, and of 'focal time-tables' grouped around some theme or project. General courses of this kind were very rare in boys' schools, where the 'new and important element in the sixth form' were hardly catered for at all. One estimate put the total number of general courses for boys in the late 1930s as no higher than eighty, the majority of these being in independent schools (*T.E.S.*, 15 March 1941 and 30 August 1941).

Pressures towards specialization

Clear ideas of what sixth-form work ought to be were poorly reflected in practice. 'Excessive and narrow specialization' was the conventional criticism. The weight of specialized work seemed too much both for effective

41

general studies and for the general courses that many sixth formers needed. Why was the curriculum pulled out of the desired shape? Was it true, as teachers often claimed, that they were fighting the good fight, but that circumstances were against them?

1. *Lack of numbers*

The value of class teaching in the sixth form was repeatedly emphasized in official reports. Sixth formers needed the stimulus of working with others and of competing against them. It was also pointed out that the 'sixth form' was a blanket term for several distinct groups—those preparing for university degrees, for other kinds of higher education, and for immediate employment—who ought not to be taught the same things in the same way. Unless schools were prepared for a substantial exchange of older pupils, as they clearly were not, these were incompatible demands. The majority of grammar schools had fewer than 400 children, so that total numbers in a typical sixth form were no higher than 20 or 30. Many found it impossible in most subjects to separate even first- and second-year sixth formers. What hope was there of any more sophisticated division? At one extreme was the Manchester Grammar School, able in 1931 to provide five distinct academic courses and a one-year commercial course for those leaving at 17. At the other was the small rural grammar school which might have no regular time-table at all for the sixth form, and might have to depend on almost individual tuition of those few who stayed on. In between were the great majority of schools which had to teach their sixth formers as a unit, gearing the work to the highest level required. This explains why scholarships taken by a few could dominate the work of many others.

2. *University scholarships*

'It is no exaggeration to say that the whole work of successful schools is primarily directed to giving able boys the best possible chance of winning open scholarships . . . the rare and refreshing fruit that the schools hope to gather' (J.E., January 1935, 5). This was the view of Cyril Norwood, from the great height of headmaster of Harrow. His concept of 'successful schools' was extremely narrow, but when university grants were so scarce, these scholarships were valuable prizes which brought prestige to the scholar and his school. They were awarded on examinations over which teachers had no control. Competition for them was seen as a major cause of intensive specialization because standards were high and very few were for work in more than one subject. 'The bulk of general papers', it was claimed, 'go into the waste-paper basket, and do not affect the ultimate award'; true or not, if this was believed in the schools, then mere lip service would be paid to the candidate's general education. Since scholarships for girls were so few, complaints were particularly fierce that the examinations gave too much scope to surface brilliance and mental gymnastics. As a general corrective, universities were often asked to consider school records, out-of-school activities and 'character as revealed in interviews', as well as formal academic achievement.

Only a minority of grammar schools were involved in the race for Oxford and Cambridge awards. But it was a growing minority, and the presence of even a few sixth formers with ambitions in this direction could influence a whole school's work. Was it possible to devise a course providing a sound general education for those leaving at 17 or 18 which would allow others to win a scholarship a year or so later? Some grammar school headmasters seemed convinced that special preparation had to begin early to give their pupils any real chance in competition with those from the public schools. State scholarships too were relatively generous in amount and brought prestige to the successful. Since they were awarded for outstanding results in the Higher Certificate examination, work in more than one subject was taken into account. But with fifteen candidates for each scholarship, the level of knowledge and sophistication required was considerable, encouraging concentration on a narrow field of study.

An important aspect of the scholarship system was its effect on the fortunes of different subjects. Latin and Greek were exceptionally well provided for, which explains the fanatical attention paid them at St. Paul's School in Compton Mackenzie's time. Even in 1937 there were more open awards in Classics at Oxford and Cambridge than in any other subject, and more than twice the number of Mathematics. English, Geography, and Biology compared with the other Sciences, were all badly served. State scholarships did something to redress the balance, though being awarded in proportion to the total number of Higher Certificate entries in each subject, they worked more to the advantage of those already established than of those, like Geography, still fighting for their place. Schools had to consider these factors when deciding which subjects to make optional and which to give prominence to in their top streams and their sixth forms.

3. *Higher School Certificate and university entry*

The new system of external examinations introduced in 1917 provided the grammar schools with clearly defined targets which influenced the whole of their work. It has been argued, indeed, that curriculum development between

44

the wars 'was left largely in the hands of the Secondary School Examinations Council and its powerful examining boards' (Montgomery, 1965, 72). Teachers' organizations were represented on the Council, and many teachers, of course, served as examiners. But there were frequent complaints that the universities had too much control over secondary education, which was being stereotyped along narrow academic lines. University influence was obviously strongest at sixth-form level. Though not an indispensable entry qualification until the end of this period, most faculties came to demand Higher Certificate passes, and were therefore vitally concerned with the content and standard of the examination. That they demanded a high level of specialized knowledge reflected the degree structure of English universities—only three years study for most students, the relative scarcity of general and of pass degrees, the dominance of single-subject courses. Higher Certificate was also used to select state scholars, and by most local authorities in making awards; in both cases, competition made high marks essential.

It was illogical to complain that such use of a 'school examination' was distorting the curriculum. It was precisely *because* the Higher Certificate was so accepted by universities, local authorities and employers that it had such value as a target and incentive. But doubts grew as to whether a single examination could provide both a suitable test of two years' post-Matriculation work for the average sixth former, *and* a means of selection for university places and awards. The headmaster of Leeds Grammar School, for example, considered that everyone who worked 'reasonably well' deserved a Certificate, because it was 'sad to fail when the standards set were those of the scholarship candidates' (*H.R.*, March 1935, 71). One obvious solution was to set special papers, or at least questions, for those competing

45

for scholarships, but to base these on the same syllabus to avoid complicating the schools' task. This was done by the Northern Board in 1938. A more drastic change was recommended in the Norwood Report. A new examination should be taken for the single purpose of selecting those of 'high intellectual distinction' clearly fit for a university, and those of 'good intellectual attainment' who might be over-strained by a severely competitive test but were likely to profit from a higher education. The recommendations of the examining boards would be considered by panels of teachers and university and local authority representatives, who would conduct interviews and consult school records. Those finally selected would receive grants from the government sufficient to allow them a full part in university life. Local authorities could still make additional awards as they saw fit. With the process of selection out of the way, a second examination could then provide a genuine leaving certificate, a clear uncompetitive record of two years advanced work. Those not concerned with university scholarships need only take this other examination, and so be saved from unduly specialized and ambitious courses (Norwood, 1943, 39-42). Sixth formers are still waiting for this salvation.

4. *Traditional assumptions about sixth-form work*

Alarm at excessive specialization and concern for the less academic sixth former whose needs were so often neglected—these were fixed points in the long debate about the sixth-form curriculum. Outside pressures were usually given as reasons why the schools could not do as they saw fit. But strong as these pressures were, the victims were not altogether unwilling. Specialization at this level seemed almost a natural law, and suggestions for a broader examination or an Intermediate Certificate brought cries of alarm that the very foundation of the sixth form was being threatened. Some degree of specialization was so widely accepted as an introduction to 'serious study' that it was difficult to argue convincingly for real alternatives. For example, any lowering of the pass standard to make possible a wider range of subjects was rejected because it would 'undermine the whole conception of sixth-form work' (S.S.E.C. Report, 1939). As was pointed out in the Norwood Report, this general view of the sixth form rested partly on certain assumptions derived from the public and older grammar schools—that sixth formers were the academic and social elite of their schools and that the universities were their true destination. Rising numbers and new courses were already fitting uneasily into the traditional academic mould. But expansion was slow, and the sixth forms of 1939 were not so different from those of twenty years before.

4

The explosion in sixth-form numbers

Secondary education after 1944

In 1944 the provision of secondary education for all became the urgent task of education authorities. What forms this second stage should take were not defined beyond the broad directive of schooling suited to 'age, aptitude and ability'. Argument and experiment were therefore invited. But the new Ministry of Education did not leave the debate open for long. Although the 1945 Labour Party conference demanded that new secondary schools should be multilateral wherever possible, official circulars advised local authorities to plan for three types of school. A pamphlet on *The Nation's Schools* (1945) was withdrawn after protests that it took tripartitism for granted. But this was only a tactical retreat, for *The New Secondary Education* (1947) described a system of schools clearly differing 'in what they teach and how they teach it', in length of course and in the balance between 'books and activities'. Multilateral schools might work best where population was scattered, but their virtues were described far more curtly than were their disadvantages. 'Past experience suggests that schools with a limited and well-defined aim are the most likely to succeed in reaching and maintaining the highest standards within the particular field they serve'. The grammar

48

schools, then, were to be highly selective, taking the top
15 per cent or so of the age group.

The minority who saw comprehensive education as vital
to post-war regeneration were soon disappointed. Briefly,
however, the grammar schools seemed 'in danger', and
educational journals 1945-7 contain a fierce debate over
their future. It was a debate in which the two sides rarely
met on common ground. Supporters of comprehensive
schools stressed their social purpose, the destruction of class
barriers. Defenders of the grammar schools concentrated
on their academic virtues, 'those standards of scholarship
and sixth-form work' which they had built up. And despite
the alarm, their position was secure. Demand for places
in grammar schools increased their intake to about 20 per
cent of the age group, a national average which concealed
indefensible variations between different parts of the
country. They were also urged repeatedly by the Minister
of Education to concentrate on the extended education of
the academically inclined, and to plan for most of their
pupils a continuous course from 11 to 18.

Sixth-form numbers

Some extravagant claims were made for the grammar
schools in face of what was described in Parliament in
1951 as 'the extremely important crisis' of early leaving.
A quarter of all grammar school leavers were under 16, and
the same proportion left without sitting the School Certificate examination, supposedly the natural climax of a
general academic education. Because the problem was
believed to have worsened since the war, the Central
Advisory Council was asked to investigate those factors
influencing the leaving age, and the 'desirability of increasing the number staying on, especially to the age of 18'. It

produced depressing evidence of wasted ability. In 1953, 10,000 boys and 5,000 girls completed advanced courses in grammar schools; in the opinion of their teachers, another 5,000 boys and 5,000 girls could have done so 'with profit' to themselves and the country (Ministry of Education, *Early Leaving*, 1954, 10). A high demand for juvenile labour, high wages, low maintenance allowances, the persistence of 'low' views of what a grammar school education meant—all these contributed to the loss of talent. The schools still seemed to be struggling to establish a four- or five-year course of general education as a minimum target for their entrants.

Sixth-form numbers had risen slowly in the 1930s, more through a larger intake into grammar schools than from any steady trend to longer school life. Soon after the war there were reports that sixth forms were growing more rapidly, but few expected the increases apparent some years later. Compare these comments, written twenty years apart: 'The great majority of grammar school pupils leave round about 16 . . . it is unusual for more than a third to reach the sixth form'; and—'In a good boys' school in a residential area, not less than 75 per cent of the entry can be expected to enter the sixth form' (Davies, 1945, 3; 1965, 130). Even allowing for the good school and the residential area, the contrast is striking. The total number of 17-year olds at school in England and Wales has more than trebled since 1947. So has the number leaving school with at least one subject passed at an advanced level. In 1939 a sixth form of 10-20 was normal. The average is now almost 120 in grammar schools, over 80 in all types of secondary school. These are the bare bones of a process which has transformed the work and character of sixth forms.

The 'bulge' and the 'trend'

One obvious reason for growth is the post-war rise in the birth rate. This had fallen during the inter-war years to a point well below replacement level in 1933, bringing alarmed forecasts of a dwindling and ageing population, and references to a 'parents' revolt' and to 'reproductive failure'. The fall was common to most industrial societies. So was the revival after the war. In this country the empty classrooms prophesied in the 1930s were soon bursting with a suddenly enlarged intake which created huge problems as it moved through the school system. The Crowther Report was written 'on the eve of a great flood', for the number of 17-year-olds increased 1959-65 by 35 per cent. And it recommended raising the school leaving age to 16 in the late 1960s when there would be a trough between two peaks of this tidal wave. Since the provision of grammar school places kept pace with the size of the age group, the number of 14-year-olds in grammar schools rose from 89,000 in 1947 to 136,000 in 1962. Other things being equal, sixth forms were bound to grow.

But other things were not equal. By 1955 a trend towards longer school life was apparent, and the Home Universities' Conference of that year discussed its implications. Some speakers argued that the universities need not prepare for it because it was only a passing phase—the 'trend' could not coincide with the 'bulge' because schools would be unable to cope with the larger intake and parents with the extra expense. Others dismissed this as complacent, calling existing plans for university expansion 'fantastically in-adequate'. The trend might well prove the more important reason for growth, and those born after the war could not be served badly simply because they were 'a tiresome generation for the planners to handle' (H.U.C. *Report*, 1955, 85-99).

This debate is mentioned because 1955 marked the beginning of the 'explosion'. Sixth-form numbers doubled over the next ten years. The total of 17-year-olds in maintained schools represented 5 per cent of the age group in 1955, almost 12 per cent in 1966. It was noted in the 1954 Report on Early Leaving that grammar schools could not visualize half their intake staying on into the sixth form, even in the most favourable conditions. Yet more than half did so ten years later. It is clear from the table that the 'trend' not only continued but intensified during the 'bulge' years, putting heavy pressure on the schools and creating fierce competition at the point of entry to higher education.

Pupils in grammar schools, aged 17 and over

Boys	Aged 17	Aged 17 as % 14-yr olds three yrs earlier	Aged 18 & over	Aged 18 as % 14-yr olds four yrs earlier
1951	11,145	24·6	5,575	11·0
1955	14,201	29·6	7,039	13·0
1959	18,060	38·6	9,851	17·6
1963	26,136	49·5	14,367	21·7
1966	34,350	54·8	17,451	25·9
Girls				
1951	10,427	22·7	2,827	6·1
1955	13,311	27·6	3,824	7·4
1959	15,218	31·8	4,734	9·2
1963	20,849	38·9	6,436	11·4
1966	28,838	46·7	10,057	14·6

Reasons for the growth of sixth forms

Highly industrialized societies depend upon long periods of formal education. But not all the forces of change are on the side of prolonged schooling. For more than twenty years in this country, juvenile unemployment has been slight.

The wages of young workers have risen faster than the average for the whole labour force, tempting advertisers to concentrate heavily on the adolescent consumer. There are many opportunities of earning good money quickly, and the desire or 'need' to do so is an important reason for early leaving. Obviously, need must be interpreted very differently in an affluent society compared with the depressed areas of the 1930s. The early sophistication of adolescents makes traditional school restraints more irksome. An important aspect of this sophistication is the trend towards earlier marriage. But though marriage may seem more important than a career to many older girls, this may be outweighed by the growing acceptance of careers for women which child rearing need only temporarily interrupt.

Despite these other influences, the balance of social change has clearly favoured educational advance. Full employment and relative prosperity make parents more willing and able to keep their children at school. They tend anyway to want more education for them than they received themselves, so that greater opportunities for one generation are more than justified in the next. This growing interest in education has been reinforced by the closer association of educational achievement with future occupation and status. As the 'bulge' years moved on to the labour market, the supply of young workers exceeded demand in some industries, limiting prospects of immediately rewarding employment. At the same time, the rising proportion of managerial and professional jobs has emphasized the value of that academic education traditionally linked to them. There is a growing demand for formal qualifications even in jobs where the need for them is less obvious, while the widening range of occupational possibilities in a 'technological society' keeps many at school and college to delay

53

a final choice as long as possible.

This has been only the barest summary of social change. Two factors of crucial importance to sixth forms will now be considered in some detail: the market value of Advanced level qualifications, and the rapid expansion in higher education.

The sixth form and careers

Of those 18-year-olds leaving maintained grammar schools in 1965-6, 70 per cent boys and 83 per cent girls went on to some form of full-time further education. This was a much higher proportion than in 1938. But enough leave the sixth form for employment to raise the old question of the vocational value of a sixth-form course in itself. There were many doubts about this in the inter-war period, and the uncertainty continued into the 1950s. Too few firms seemed to accept A-level qualifications as a foothold on at least the second rung of the ladder, or to pay these older recruits anything extra. Conditions of entry at 16 and 18 were too similar in many occupations, both in pay and promotion prospects (M. of E., *Early Leaving*, 1954, 49-53).

Yet the situation was clearly improving. In 1950 the Headmasters' Employment Committee reported that the 'ever rising standards of academic and personal qualities required by both commercial and industrial firms' indicated that far more boys ought to stay on at school. In 1955 a system of student apprenticeships was introduced for boys entering industry with A-level passes in mathematics and science; this was later extended to girls, and to some from the Arts side. An inquiry by the I.A.A.M. four years later showed better opportunities and some financial advantages for older leavers in a wide range of occupations. Except for technical jobs, the particular subjects studied at school seemed less important than evidence of a capacity for further training, and the experience of responsibility provided in a sixth form.

There is an obvious 'snowball effect' at work here. More stay on as the value of doing so becomes apparent. As sixth forms grow, employers are forced to 'wait for the best'. More emphasis on paper qualifications means higher barriers at entry, and 'the educational history of the last twenty years has been punctuated every few weeks by a faint click as some new professional body established a new training course or raised its entry standards' (*T.E.S.*, 8 January 1965, 58). In many occupations traditionally recruited from grammar schools, the officer class is expanding rapidly at the expense of the rank and file. In others, high qualifications may be demanded as a sign of their status, or as proof of their attractiveness, or as a way of keeping out the socially unsuitable. Part of this process has been an increasing emphasis on A-level passes, rather than O-level alone, as a preliminary to, or substitute for, professional examinations. A-level passes are a positive advantage in entry to banking and insurance. They are required by, for example, the Law and Pharmaceutical Societies; for admission to the R.A.F. College at Cranwell and to engineering apprenticeships in Civil Aviation; for direct entry into competition for the Civil Service Executive Class; for entry to many sandwich courses in industry and to some famous teaching hospitals for nurses. A survey of over 2,000 Joint Matriculation Board candidates who left school for work in 1963 with at least two A-level passes showed the boys going mainly to industrial apprenticeships, management training, banking, accountancy, insurance, pharmacy, the Civil Service and local government. Girls went mainly to Civil Service and secretarial work, librarianship, pharmacy, and to nursing and other medical services

(Lawrence, 1964). In most of these occupations, entry at sixteen offers only routine posts unless qualifications are made up later. But in most of them too, it is entry at graduate level which offers the major prizes. The demand for degree or equivalent qualifications is rising rapidly in many branches of, e.g., engineering, management and the professions. And though the prospects of sixth-form leavers have greatly improved since the early 1950s, it is the passport to higher education that remains the most obvious benefit of a sixth-form course.

Growth in higher education

The number of undergraduates in British universities rose from 50,000 in 1938 to over 150,000 in 1966. This represents a major social revolution, providing an elite constantly renewed and enlarged. The first move forward followed the war, when the urgent needs of ex-servicemen reinforced the general zeal for reform. Student numbers reached a record 89,000 in 1949, bringing reports of accommodation strained to the limit and fears of a decline in standards if numbers continued to rise. Ten years later, with the 'bulge' approaching the universities and the 'trend' confirmed, the Crowther Committee wrote of an imminent crisis as the provision of places fell far behind the demand from those 'qualified' to fill them. The demand for rapid expansion in the Robbins Report (1963) was not based on utilitarian forecasts of manpower needs but on the principle that 'higher education should be available for all those qualified by ability and attainment to pursue it, and who wish to do so' (Robbins, 8). Though estimates of future demand were widely criticized as too low, this was a clear rejection of any narrow restriction of entry. Robbins's short-term targets were reached, the number admitted to degree courses in 1966 exceeding the total of all university students thirty years before.

Supply had met demand in the 1930s partly because the career advantages of a degree were less apparent, partly because of the high barrier of cost. There were places for those who could afford them. Grants and scholarships were too few and unfairly distributed, and after the war a more egalitarian and efficient system was demanded. The maximum value of a state scholarship was raised so as to cover, in theory, the whole cost of a degree course; local authorities were advised to do the same with grants; and university open scholarships were supplemented by the government to the full value of a state scholarship. In 1948 an official working party on university awards urged that no one should be denied higher education by lack of means. Twelve years later the Anderson Report on *Grants to Students* (M. of E.) argued that all those accepted by universities deserved support from public funds, subject only to a means test. The now fashionable idea of student loans was firmly rejected. It was being claimed that since higher education usually meant higher earnings, the wholesale subsidizing of students would create a new form of social privilege. But grants were not charity, they were a matter of national self-interest. Loans would mean an 'untimely burden' of debt at the outset of a career. And since so many potential students came from homes with little experience of prolonged education, it was vital to remove fears of financial liability.

Action on this report was prompt. From September 1962 grants had to be paid by local authorities to all those with at least two A-level passes who were admitted to degree or comparable courses. Grants could also be given to those with lower qualifications or taking courses at a lower level. State scholarships were abolished as no longer necessary.

The extent of these changes can be seen from the proportion of university students assisted from public funds—41 per cent in 1938, 80 per cent in 1956, 98 per cent in 1963.

'Fit for admission, fit for aid', means that competition for the means to go to university is no longer a source of tension in sixth-form work. It has been replaced by competition for places. In 1957 three-quarters of those with the minimum entrance requirements were admitted to university courses. In 1961 the proportion was only 61 per cent. In October 1967, 50,000 students began their university work while another 31,000 applicants with the minimum of two A-level passes had been rejected. This pressure on places has become the major influence on advanced work in schools, and will be discussed in the next chapter. Despite the temptation to feel that only those accepted are really suitable, it is clear that many who could have gained a university place with ease ten years ago are now disappointed. And since there is no absolute called 'a university education' which cannot be diluted, it is a matter of policy, not a law of nature, to exclude them.

Though the problem will remain as long as there is a wide gap in status between universities and 'the rest', pressure has eased in recent years through the rapid expansion of other forms of higher education. Colleges of Education (formerly called training colleges) have long been a major outlet for sixth formers, taking twice as many girls as did the universities in 1938. With the schools multiplying their demands for staff, the colleges have been transformed in size, scope, and status. The number of entrants rose from 13,000 in 1956 to 34,000 ten years later, while the prospect of degrees in education increased their attractiveness as alternatives to the universities. Also of importance to sixth forms has been the change in their entry requirements. In the 1930s the colleges did not normally expect Higher Certificate qualifications, and so allowed their entrants to take general courses at school free from examination pressure. In 1966 almost half their entrants had two or more A-level passes, and two years in a sixth form was a normal preliminary to teacher training. The expansion of technical colleges, too, has a far greater importance for sixth forms than as an alternative for those falling out of the university race. Many undoubtedly do degrees there as a second best. But the 'steady tramp of sixth formers to full-time further education' is partly explained by the clear vocational purpose of many of the courses, the close links with industry, and the widening opportunities to work for a degree (Armytage, 1968, 25). Sixth forms now prepare for a far more varied system of higher education, and this has obvious implications for their work.

Entry to higher education from state-aided grammar schools, 1965-6

% leavers going to:		university	colleges of education	other full-time further ed.	All forms higher ed.
Boys	Aged 17	23	2	12	37
	" 18	44	7	15	66
	" 19	40	15	19	74
Girls	Aged 17	11	12	18	41
	" 18	27	33	14	74
	" 19	33	38	9	80

The pool of ability

The steep rise in sixth-form and college numbers inevitably brought fears that 'more means worse'. But estimates of what proportion of a population can benefit from prolonged education are cultural judgments, reflecting what a particular society at a particular time needs or will provide. In this country, 1 per cent 17-year-olds were receiving full-time education in 1870, 2 per cent in 1902, 4 per cent in

1938, and 15 per cent in 1962. The proportion of this age group still at school in the early 1960s was higher in Sweden than France, in France than Britain, in Britain than Germany—and these countries are at a comparable stage of industrialization. Less than one in ten went on to higher education in Britain compared with one in three in the United States. It is an interesting example of changing attitudes that Michael Sadler, known for his 'progressive' ideas on education, saw pressure of numbers threatening the quality of university work almost forty years ago (*T.E.S.*, 21 February 1931, 70). If there are genetic limits to the pool of ability, they are so far away as to be safely ignored. What *is* important now is the wastage of ability, the preoccupation of every major educational report since 1954. A large-scale survey in 1958, for example, showed that 42 per cent of the top ability group had left school at or before the age of sixteen (Crowther, 1959, 409). And striking though the 'trend' may have been, less than half the grammar school leavers of 1966 had taken A-level, and less than a fifth entered universities—this from an intake thought capable at 11 of a prolonged academic education. The whole concept of a pool of ability must be vague because of the immeasurable gap between the actual and the potential. There are so many 'whose entry into higher education depends greatly on how they have lived and been taught beforehand' (Robbins, 1963, 49). Some of these differences will now be considered.

1. *Differences between schools in size of sixth forms*

Even within the same area, schools differ widely in quality of teaching, the range of courses they offer, and in the extent to which entry to the sixth form is taken for granted by staff, pupils and parents. They also differ in the freedom they allow, both before and in the sixth form. Since the rejection of school restraints is an important reason for leaving early, this affects the size of their sixth forms. These are intangible differences. But some statistical generalizations can be made. Sixth forms are larger *proportionately* in direct grant schools; 65 per cent of their 14-year-old pupils in 1961 were still at school three years later, compared with 53 per cent in maintained grammar schools. They are larger proportionately in large schools, urban schools, and boys' schools. The reasons are closely interwoven. Direct-grant schools tend to be more socially and intellectually selective. Rural schools tend to be small and rural areas tend to contain a high proportion of manual workers. Fewer girls stay on than boys, while mixed schools until recently have tended to be in country districts, housing estates and new towns rather than in middle-class suburbs.

Small schools face obvious difficulties in organizing sixth-form work. First- and second-year sixths may have to be taught together. There are fewer special allowances to attract well qualified staff. Choice of subjects may be very limited, and co-operation between schools to fill the gaps is not always popular or practicable. Despite the overall rise in sixth-form numbers, advanced work can still be wildly uneconomic. A survey of northern grammar schools in 1966 showed three with fewer than 25 in the sixth form, eleven with fewer than 50, and only eight with more than 150. The range of subjects varied from eighteen in the largest to twelve in the smallest, with some subjects being taken by only one or two (D.E.S., *Trends in Education* No. 7, 1967). For this reason alone, educational opportunities may be determined by the accident of residence, especially in rural areas, and there have been demands for the concentration of advanced work in selected schools (with boarding accommodation provided), or for the integration of public schools in the state system as sixth-form centres for those otherwise deprived of suitable provision.

2. *Regional differences in size of sixth forms*

There are large regional differences in the proportion staying on at school, differences which may reflect 'the local employment pattern and the scale of educational provision, not the needs of the children' (Crowther, 1959, 10). In south-east England in 1966, almost 15 per cent 17-year-olds were still in secondary schools. The proportion was higher in Wales (17 per cent) but lower in all other regions; in the North and in East Anglia it was below 10 per cent. To give more detailed examples, the figures in 1960 ranged in the counties from 28 per cent in Cardiganshire to 6 per cent in Lincolnshire, in the county boroughs from 15 per cent in Merthyr and Bath to under 3 per cent in West Ham and Bury.

Much of the explanation lies in the social character of different areas, the balance between various occupational groups. There have been wide differences too in the provision of grammar school places. The higher this is, the larger the *proportion* staying on into the sixth form. The influence of local employment prospects is also strong, even though grammar school pupils tend to range more widely than their contemporaries in search of jobs. Those areas out of the main stream of economic activity offer less well-paid employment to young workers, and the high proportion of early leavers in parts of the Midlands reflects the lure of the car industry. The South-east offers so many openings in professional and administrative work that the material rewards of prolonged education are especially

62

obvious. Conventional attitudes to staying on are another powerful influence. Wales, where the ratio of older pupils is greatest, is traditionally credited with a high regard for education and the 'learned professions'. It has also been most generously provided with grammar school places.

3. Sixth-form boys and girls

Investigation of 'wasted' ability has concentrated on the connection between social class and educational opportunity. Too little attention has been paid to the large number of girls who end their formal education too early. The crucial period for this 'wastage' is from 16-18. There is little difference in the number of boys and girls taking O-level. But only eight girls to every ten boys stay at school until 18, and only a third as many girls leave with three passes at A-level. The Robbins Committee saw a vital reserve of ability here which the country could not afford to lose, and believed that prejudice against 'over-educating' girls was being steadily overcome. Despite their optimism, however, the gap between the number of boys and girls entering sixth forms widened in the period 1961-6.

There are organizational reasons for this. The shortage of well qualified staff is more acute in girls' schools, and in science subjects they are desperately scarce. Only half as many girls take O-level before they are sixteen, so fewer can afford three years in a sixth form. Women are outnumbered three to one at the universities, though it has been claimed that fewer still would be admitted were it not for some favourable treatment in marks and interviews (Ollerenshaw, 1961, 135-9). There are broader reasons too. Older girls may find a traditional school atmosphere particularly irksome. They may still be less career-conscious than boys, and far more of them marry before they are twenty. Differences in leaving age between children of manual and non-manual parents are greater for girls, suggesting less willingness to make sacrifices for them or to encourage their ambitions.

4. *Social selection in secondary education*

Equality of opportunity was the great hope of the 1944 Education Act. Age, aptitude and ability were to determine the education provided, while tests used for selection and guidance were to penetrate the masking effects of an unfavourable home environment. But there was no parity of esteem between secondary schools of different types. And measured ability was itself so closely related to social background that the grammar schools remained predominantly middle-class schools. The process of social selection continues and intensifies during the years 11-16, making the sixth form far less socially mixed than is the main school. This process has been so extensively documented that only the barest outline can be given here.

The *Early Leaving* Report (1954), the first educational report to be based on a social survey, showed that those borderline grammar school entrants who went on to successful sixth-form work were drawn overwhelmingly from professional and managerial homes. Of promising entrants who deteriorated markedly, over 90 per cent came from the homes of unskilled or semi-skilled workers. In the Crowther social survey, 62 per cent grammar school pupils from professional and managerial homes had left over the age of 17, compared with 28 per cent whose fathers were skilled manual workers and only 15 per cent whose fathers were semi-skilled or unskilled (Vol. 2, 17). How independent such differences could be even of

measured ability was shown clearly in the Robbins Report
(Appendix 1, 38).

Highest level of education reached by children born 1940-1

I.Q. range	Social background	Degree level %	G.C.E. A-level only %
130+	non-manual	37	7
	manual	18	14
115-129	non-manual	17	17
	manual	8	10

There is no evidence that these inequalities have been
reduced in recent years. Their explanation has been looked
for in peer-group influences and in parental behaviour,
values and expectations. Little attention yet has been paid
to those school demands to which children respond very
differently according to their background and previous
experience. Some of these may create unnecessary barriers
to learning.

Once in the sixth form the worst hurdles are past, at
least for boys, and attempts to relate university achievement to home background have been dismissed as unconvincing because students 'are already so highly selected
in terms of that very factor' (Furneaux, 1961, 68).
Certainly, sixth formers from working-class homes do as
well at A-level as their contemporaries, and there are no
significant differences at the degree stage either. The main
'wastage' occurs before or at the point of entry to the sixth
form. It seems strange, then, that maintenance allowances
for sixth formers have been the cinderella of the grants
system. Financial need may be only one reason for early
leaving, but it is more easily visible and more easily
remedied than most. Official circulars in 1945 and 1949
emphasized that such allowances were to be used only as
a last resort, and could neither replace possible earnings
nor relieve the general poverty of a family. The *Early*

65

Leaving Report (1954) rejected any scheme for selective sixth-form scholarships, but called for an immediate increase in allowances to offset the rising level of juvenile wages. They were increased in 1957. The raising of the age limit for income-tax allowances for dependent children to 18 was some help, but even when this is included, the support given to sixth formers from poor homes falls well below that given to university students living at home (*T.E.S.*, 1 December 1967).

5. *Recruitment from a narrow selective base*

The fallibility of selection at 11 has long been accepted. Yet even in 1958, 95 per cent of all pupils aged 17 were in state-aided or independent grammar schools. Late entrants to grammar schools fell very far below the number capable of profiting from advanced work, and there were few opportunities of it outside them. The 'great expansion' of sixth forms that had taken place had been on 'the relatively small and fixed base of those already in selective schools' (Crowther, 1959, 229). The broadening of this base during the next ten years, discussed in the last chapter, has transformed the scope of sixth-form work. It has also enlarged the 'pool of ability'.

5

The sixth-form curriculum, 1944-68

'There is an educational theory behind School Certificate, even if the theory may be imperfect. . . . But when School Certificate has been passed, theory collapses before the imperious pressure of examination.' This was Sir Richard Livingstone's comment in 1947 (Universities' Quarterly, Vol. 1, No. 3, p.245), the year in which the whole system of secondary school examinations was recast. The theory behind School Certificate was of a balanced general education, and the insistence on passes in certain subjects was an attempt to guarantee it. The sixth-form curriculum was founded on the intensive study of a few subjects, supported by more general work. Under the pressure of competition for grants and scholarships this general work was usually neglected.

The reform of external examinations was in the air long before 1947. The Norwood Committee suggested abolishing them altogether before the age of 18, and introducing two quite separate sixth-form examinations—one to select university scholars and one to provide a genuine leaving certificate. Early reactions suggested that the advice might be followed. But the proposals announced in 1947 and put into operation four years later involved a less radical change.

The General Certificate of Education

The new Certificate was offered at three levels. The Ordinary level provided a 'reasonable test' of work done 'as part of a wide and general secondary course up to the age of *at least* sixteen'. There were no grades of pass, no insistence on particular subjects. The Advanced level examined work studied intensively during two years in a sixth form, the old subsidiary standard being abolished. Again, the choice of subjects was to be as free as school time-tabling and university requirements allowed. A further Scholarship level gave 'specially gifted pupils an opportunity of showing distinctive merit and promise'. State scholarships and other awards could be based on it without setting unreasonable standards for the average sixth former.

In speeches and circulars the Minister of Education stressed the flexibility and freedom of the new system. Grammar schools could now plan their work as a single course with no unnatural break at 16. Since A-level passes could be awarded on Scholarship papers, and O-level passes on Advanced papers, there would be no barriers between one stage and the next. 'It would be contrary to the intentions of the system for any pupil to sit successfully for two or three levels in the same subject'. Schools could decide for each individual the right time to begin specialized work, and a pupil might take subjects at three different levels in the same year.

The aims were admirable, but were soon betrayed. The abolition of grades was attacked as 'egalitarianism gone mad' and a 'legalized concealment of merit'. Distinctions were soon introduced at A-level, but no other details were given publicly until 1963. The age limit of 16 before entry for any external examination was intended to postpone outside pressures on the curriculum, save the secondary moderns from apeing the grammar schools, and persuade some of the 25 per cent grammar school pupils who left at fifteen to stay a full five years. There was an immediate outcry that maturity could not be measured by chronological age, and that many children were being forced to mark time for a year. In 1953 heads were allowed to sanction earlier entry in *individual* cases, a concession which gave them a free hand to create express streams. The opportunity to by-pass O-level in some subjects was almost wholly neglected. Heads of department who allowed it found many dropping their subject altogether. Heads of schools who encouraged it faced the argument that since no 15-year-old could guarantee the successful completion of a sixth-form course, it was safer to acquire an impressive list of O-level passes even if some of them were in subjects taken again at A-level. In practice, then, those beginning advanced work early have usually done so after taking eight or more subjects at O-level in four years.

The Advanced-level has been a subject examination, the subjects neither gathered into groups nor combined into coherent courses. On the science side they may be 'mutually supportive'. On the arts side, they show none of that 'organic unity' demanded of sixth-form courses in 1917, and have been described by a recent committee of headmasters as 'three elongated, parallel and unconnected pseudo-specialisms, three feeble prongs scratching at the surface of thought' (H.M.A., The Sixth Form of the Future, 1968, II). The range of subjects offered has widened considerably since the 1930s, with the introduction of, for example, more foreign languages, economic history, sociology, political studies, technical drawing, metalwork and woodwork. These have done something to meet

69

criticism of a bias towards literary culture and pure science. But there are still gaps. Technology is badly under-represented and commercial subjects are still regarded suspiciously as unsuitable for academic examination. The rapid increase in 'new sixth formers' is now stimulating more vocational courses, while a Schools Council working party is considering the whole relationship of A-level examinations to commercial and industrial needs. Radical changes may therefore be imminent. What has long been apparent is the change in the fortunes of subjects. Classics, much less strongly reinforced by university entrance requirements, have declined. Modern languages have taken only a small share of the total increase in numbers. Geography has prospered and economics shown a remarkable rate of growth. But the most important change by far has been the 'swing' from science since the early 1960s.

The swing from science

To the 'bulge' and the 'trend' which already dominated discussion of secondary education in the 1950s was added the 'swing'—the growing preference among boys for the study of science. The opportunities and achievements of a scientific age seemed to be forcing arts subjects to recruit 'the weak students or the careful plodders', brightened only by the occasional 'gifted eccentric' flying in the face of fashion (Stevens, 1960, 79). Well over 60 per cent sixth-form boys in 1958 were specializing wholly in science and mathematics, and plans for university expansion assumed that the swing would continue. Yet a swing back was visible by 1963. A-level entries in those subjects were growing less rapidly, and the second report of the Universities Central Council on Admissions (U.C.C.A.) spoke of empty places in departments of science and technology even though their minimum standards for entry were 'almost without exception lower' than in arts. Between 1962 and 1966, entries through the U.C.C.A. rose by 41 per cent in pure science, 28 per cent in technology, 55 per cent in arts, and 11 per cent in social studies. Of course, figures can be misleading. Unfilled science places are largely the result of a massive expansion in science departments in the early 1960s which was not matched in other sectors of university work. Subjects like economics and sociology grew from such low bases in the 1950s that percentage increases are bound to look startling. And the numbers taking 'mixed' sixth-form courses which include some mathematics or science have risen rapidly in recent years—though as faculty requirements stand now, this will not increase the university intake in science.

Even when all the extenuating circumstances are admitted, the situation seems odd in a 'technological society'. It led the Council for Scientific Policy to commission a detailed investigation into the swing. The interim report, in 1965, was fairly reassuring. The final report three years later was thoroughly alarmist. Though the number of sixth formers taking science was still increasing each year, the proportion doing so was declining so rapidly that numbers would soon fall unless remedies were found. Various explanations were given. The aridity of many science syllabuses made the subject seem remote from human problems at the very time when interest in social and cultural studies was growing. Careers in science still seemed relatively unattractive outside the world of pure research, and rewards in industry seemed greater on the managerial than on the technical side (Dainton, 1968, 28-32). There was a shortage of graduate teachers in mathematics and science. This was especially true in girls' schools, and reinforced the arts bias of sixth-form girls. In summer 1966, for example, nearly 60 per cent A-level entries in English and French were from girls, compared with only about 15 per cent in mathematics and physics. Most important of all, perhaps, and certainly most removable, were the effects of premature and narrow specialization. This faced many with a choice between arts and science before they had been taught by science specialists at all, and forced those choosing science to abandon all serious study of the other side. Among the remedies proposed was a drastic broadening of sixth-form work to cover five equal subjects spanning the 'two cultures' (Dainton, 1968, 85). This was one of many recent rejections of sixth-form specialization.

Main subjects at A-level: number of passes, and % all A-level passes

	Summer 1956		Summer 1960		Summer 1966	
Subject	No.	%	No.	%	No.	%
English	11,462	11	14,565	10	31,850	12
Latin	49,441	5	4,910	3	5,911	2
French	8,328	8	10,277	7	18,497	7
German	2,247	2	3,102	2	5,561	2
History	10,004	9	12,230	8	23,103	9
Geography	6,256	6	7,665	5	17,645	7
Economics*	2,944	3	5,575	4	17,501	7
Mathematics	15,773	15	26,858	18	40,772	16
Physics	14,382	14	20,519	14	28,856	11
Chemistry	11,964	11	16,605	11	21,582	8
Biology	3,323	3	3,772	3	9,049	3

% increase in number of A-level passes

Subject	1956-60	1963-6
English	28	59
French	23	37
History	22	38
Geography	25	53
Economics	89	64
Mathematics	70	25
Physics	43	15
Chemistry	39	11
Biology	14	57

Specialization

'When a pupil enters the sixth form, he becomes a specialist . . . the subjects of his serious intellectual study are confined to two or three' (Crowther, 1959, 257). This has been the normal pattern, rarely altered in boys' schools except by the large number taking *four* subjects at A-level —a practice usually condemned as making real study in depth impossible. Even for sixth-form girls, general courses dwindled in the 1950s as entry requirements for teaching and other occupations were raised. It is only in recent years that this pattern has been seriously questioned, and sixth-form work become much more varied in scope.

Traditionally, the foundation of advanced work in schools has been a rigorous training in a few subjects. In both the degree of concentration and the total separation of arts and science which is possible, this country is unique. 'Subject mindedness' has seemed the hall-mark of a keen sixth former, ready at 15 or 16 to tackle some aspect of human knowledge 'with all the one-sided enthusiasm of the young' (Crowther, 1959, 258f.). Yet his contemporaries in other countries are either less single-minded, or are being forcibly fed a different diet. Specialization in the French *baccalaureat* is a matter of emphasis within a wide course, so that even in his last year at school the mathematician studies philosophy, a modern language, history and geography. The German gymnasium student takes as many as nine subjects for the *abitur* which gives right of entry to a university. Russian secondary schools maintain a broad curriculum to the end, with no subject given more than six periods a week. In America, the idea of a general and balanced education continues into the colleges (Spolton, 1967).

There is an obvious danger in defending on principle, or

as natural, what may be the result of tradition or convenience. Writing in 1953 Eric James defended specialization because 'it allows some glimpses of real standards of achievement', and because the universities 'as we know them' assume a 'genuine standard of perform- ance' (*J.E.*, January 1953). The words 'real' and 'genuine' defy definition. Even in the Crowther Report, it is admitted that subject-mindedness is partly the result of a steady drift towards specialization in the main grammar school curriculum. Because of the necessities of time-tabling and the demands of universities, broader courses may be im- practical rather than unwanted. Thus one sixth-form survey showed that 40 per cent would have chosen to combine arts and science subjects if given the chance, compared with only 6 per cent who had been able to do so (Peterson, 1960, 8). Specialization has long been defended as having a special value which more superficial study could not possess, allowing sixth formers to learn something thoroughly enough to know what knowledge means, and giving an emotional stimulus to intellectual effort. But wide agreement on its virtues has been accom- panied by wide agreement on the dangers of carrying it too far. These dangers have become so apparent as to challenge the whole concept of 'study in depth'.

Specialization to excess

Criticism has concentrated on three points. Specialization begins too early, is excessive even in the sixth form, and involves too sharp a separation between arts and science.

In theory, advanced work rests on a firm base of four or five years general and balanced education. In practice, specialization begins well down the secondary school. Of the hundred grammar schools inspected in 1956-57, eighty had forced some choice between arts and science by the end of the third year in the interests of university entry. Their curriculum was being distorted by 'counting back' from what it seemed necessary to know at a much later stage. The result was a 'premature closing of doors' which fixed as permanent decisions 'what may be no more than passing inclinations' (Crowther, 1959, 210-4). In this narrowing process, art and music are the first victims. History and geography often follow them, being made options far earlier than in other countries. But it is the choice between science or languages which has caused most concern, forcing pupils to develop much too early along diverging lines. This explains the proposal that no main school course should contain more than two languages or two sciences. There are obvious objections to overloading the curriculum on either side, and to leaving too much to the 'uninformed and immature decisions' of 13- or 14-year-olds (Dainton, 1968, 85). It has been urged repeatedly that the options must be left open long enough to make enlightened choice possible. Yet 40 per cent of university Arts students in 1961 had taken no science at O-level, while present entry requirements for science degrees make it possible for over half of all O-level candidates to be taking combinations of subjects which put them out of the reckoning as early as 16 (Dainton, 1968, 74). Even the pre-sixth-form course, then, may be a travesty of a general education.

Once in the sixth form, the division into arts and science has usually been clear cut. Mathematics is increasingly necessary for economists, geography does something to span the gulf, and growing numbers are taking 'mixed' courses. Even so, these courses involved only 13 per cent grammar school sixth formers in 1966, compared with 36 per cent doing mathematics and science only, and 50 per cent taking neither mathematics nor science. The nearest contrast is with Scotland, where in the same year 86 per cent boys and 60 per cent girls entering universities had passes in Higher mathematics.

Complaints about overpressure have been perennial. And as in the 1930s, the accepted formula—not more than two-thirds of the timetable to be devoted to specialist studies—has been widely ignored. Indeed, the temptation to squeeze out less 'useful' work has grown stronger, with the pressure 'to show results in terms of examination achievement so intense as to seriously overload the curriculum and place general education in jeopardy' (S.S.E.C., 1960, 2). Many surveys have shown how seriously the balance has been upset, with sixth formers spending over 80 per cent of school time and over 90 per cent of all their working time on their main subjects (e.g. Peterson, 1960, 6). In its feasibility studies for Working Paper No. 5, the Schools Council found only four of its fifteen schools giving as many as six periods a week to general studies; seven gave fewer than four periods to that 'balance' and 'contrast' so long recommended as essential ingredients of sixth-form work.

Pressures on the curriculum

1. University scholarships

Competition for the means to go to university was the main pressure on sixth-form work in the 1930s. Now grants are given as a right to those accepted, and state scholarships given for distinction in two subjects have disappeared. But awards at Oxford and Cambridge colleges retain their appeal. As an influence for specialization these are established villains of the piece. Though the Crowther

Committee knew of 'no better way of choosing the ablest', it stressed that scholarship examinations ought not to be used to select for ordinary entrance, and that the field ought to be small. Yet they *are* used to select entrants, and the field is large. There are some awards for work in several subjects, and general papers are dutifully set, but it is a brilliant performance in one subject which most often carries the day. Success brings money and status to the scholar, and so much status to his school that there have been calls for an end to the annual league table which records how many the various schools have won.

Candidates from independent and direct-grant schools still dominate the field, but maintained schools have increased their share markedly in recent years. The colleges themselves have encouraged entries from schools which had previously felt themselves beyond the pale, so that far more schools are affected by the competition. In practice, this often means still more intensive teaching of main subjects. It almost certainly involves a third year in the sixth form, and so is the main stimulus to express streams and the earliest possible entry to advanced work. 'For each winner of an open award, there are two or three who have been pressed too hard' (*T.E.S.*, 6 May 1960, 902). This estimate, by a Cambridge tutor, greatly underrates the pressure.

2. *University demands*

Schools have long felt themselves at the mercy of the universities in the shaping of sixth-form work. Yet the universities themselves are under heavy pressure. Degree courses are shorter than in comparable countries and it is argued that only specialized preparation in sixth forms makes an honours degree in three years possible at all. This is why demands for some reduction of pressure on the schools include expensive suggestions for an extra year, either for all students or for those taking honours degrees. Much of what is done at degree level might be left for post-graduate work by the really academic. Another important aspect of university work in this country is the high proportion of students—nearly 70 per cent in 1963-4—taking only one main subject. Though much has been done since the Robbins Report to meet its demands for more general degrees and more joint or combined honours courses, most university work remains highly specialized. And those intermediate courses which used to introduce many university students to specialist study have largely disappeared, so that sixth forms necessarily cover work which could once have been left to the next stage. The relatively low failure rate at universities is another source of pressure on the schools. The *baccalaureat* in France and the *abitur* in Germany give the right to enter a university. In both countries, 'wastage' reduces the number actually qualifying to the British level even though the intake is considerably larger. The United States can afford to admit over 30 per cent of the age group to college because of the 'cooling-off' of those unsuited to higher education, a proportion of which may be half the intake (Clark, 1961). But British universities rely on a fine sieve before entry to reduce 'wastage' to about 15 per cent. What they demand of entrants is therefore the main influence on sixth-form work, since even those not intending entry are normally taught with those who are.

By the 1930s the battle was won to make a sixth-form course an essential preliminary to university study. Applicants had to have certain School Certificate credits as evidence of sound general education, and two or more Higher Certificate passes as proof of fitness for specialized work. The great hope of flexibility in the new G.C.E. made revision essential, for if O-level could be by-passed by able pupils, then a wide spread of subjects at that stage could no longer be demanded. How narrow a course would the universities accept, and how far would they 'trust the schools' to provide a balanced education? A trial scheme was introduced 1951-5, when minimum requirements were to be passes in English, a foreign language, mathematics or science, and two or three other subjects, with two subjects taken at A-level. Most universities accepted this, a great advance on the chaotic individualism of earlier periods. But argument continued. Universities were still inclined to want guarantees of a 'reasonably broad foundation to specialist work' because the schools needed support against all the pressures to narrow the curriculum. The schools were inclined to dismiss them as overloading the timetable without providing any real test of general education, and the tide has gone their way. Apart from English, general demands for passes in specific subjects have dwindled. The most common general requirement is for five subjects, with two at A-level, or four subjects, three at A-level. Some universities even accept three A-level passes only if one of them is in General Studies.

But general entry requirements are only the first, low, hurdle. Course requirements still vary so much between departments and faculties as to demand long annual guide-books and the presence on school staffs of some expert in the complexities of the '18-Plus'. Far more important than the variety of the hurdles, however, has been their increasing height. The severest pressure to specialize has come from the competition for university places.

3. Competition for university places

Universities 'have a right to information about the educational achievement and aptitude of their candidates which they can regard as a reasonably objective basis for comparisons' (S.C. Working Paper 16, 5). But they have had to select from rapidly growing numbers with at least the basic qualifications. The result has been a widening gap between minimum and actual entry standards, with departments asking for three or even four A-levels, specifying which are acceptable, and requiring high grades of pass. When so many more apply than can be taken, what is a fair and efficient 'basis for comparison'?

Over twenty years ago, pressure on places brought argument about the whole basis of selecting students. Yet the only major change since has been in the machinery of selection, with the setting up in 1961 of a clearing house for applications. Special entrance examinations have largely disappeared outside Oxford and Cambridge, where they are still regarded with an awe which stifles criticism. Interviews, despite consuming staff time, are of doubtful effectiveness (Himmelweit, 1963). School reports are impossible to standardize. This leaves A-level as 'the best single instrument of selection', but still a blunt one. It has so many other purposes to serve. In a feeble echo of the Norwood Report, Special Papers were introduced to test 'intellectual grasp', promise rather than achievement. But this was only tinkering with the problem, since universities can ignore them and applicants are not handicapped by not taking them. Schools have realized this, and the proportion of Special to A-level papers fell from 14 per cent in 1963 to under 10 per cent in 1967. They are obviously taken by only a minority of university entrants. The universities are left with the grades of pass, introduced in 1961 because, while the simple pass-fail-distinction was too broad, marks implied an unrealistic degree of precision in sorting out candidates. Even if reliable, A-level grades are announced too late to be used in preliminary selection except for those resitting the examination because their previous results were unacceptable. The usual procedure is therefore to offer places subject to a prescribed level of performance in the subsequent examination, and the clearing-up operation of matching applicants still unplaced with places still unfilled has to be crammed into a few weeks in September.

What grades are asked for varies with individual candidates, but varies far more strikingly with different subjects. In September 1964, most Arts faculties were refusing to consider candidates with less than two or three Bs, and some wanted As. Only in the least popular departments of science and technology were bare passes acceptable. In arts and social studies the few marks separating an A from a B in one subject may determine an applicant's fate. If a department can only take, perhaps, one in ten of those who make it their first choice, what other 'hard' facts can they use? Yet there is no clear evidence that A-level performance in a subject *is* a reliable indication of university achievement except in the very highest ability range. This is hardly surprising when university methods, atmosphere, and subject content are so different. Overall performance seems more reliable than results in specific subjects, and it has been suggested that more general courses in sixth forms, whatever their other advantages, may be a more efficient preparation for university work (Miller, 1968).

If reliance on A-level results is something of an act of faith, is there a case for academic aptitude tests such as American colleges have long used? The Robbins Committee recommended research into them, but they are still regarded with suspicion as the last refuge of those made desperate by numbers and as having a 'backwash' even more deadening for schools than traditional examinations (Albrow, 1967). This backwash effect may well be the most important factor in the situation, the Crowther Committee urging universities to put *first* what effects their demands had on schools, since all selection methods were unreliable. To demand a high level of performance in a few subjects is to encourage concentration on those subjects, intensive teaching, and the avoidance of risks. The multiplying of opportunities of higher education outside the universities may offer some release of pressure, but there is a growing tendency for colleges and professional bodies to ask for A-level passes. Increasingly 'it is specialized knowledge and skill that lead to social status and economic reward' (Oliver, 1966, 312).

The search for 'general and cultural balance' in sixth-form work

It is possible to see specialization itself as the key to general education, with the student becoming aware of the wider implications of his subject and moving out to other ground. Certainly, there are obvious dangers in dabbling, in adding a dash of culture here and a scientific antidote there to produce the right mixture. But it is generally accepted that specialization alone is not enough. What else should sixth formers do? Prescriptions are often extravagant, implying an overview of the whole of life and civilization, but some idea of the 'essentials' of any true education appears again and again. The famous Harvard Report on *General Education in a Free Society* (1946) wanted half of any student's time devoted to a common course in humanities ('Man's inner vision'), social studies and science. This is echoed by the demand that any advanced course must develop together 'all the main modes of thinking'—logical, empirical, moral and aesthetic; this suggested a four-subject sixth-form course in English, mathematics, a science, and history or a language, with additional work in religious study, music and art (Peterson, 1960, 15). Such a wide common course carried through secondary school is found in other countries. Here, outside pressures have worked against it.

The Crowther Committee made the traditional division into specialist subjects taking just over half school time; complementary studies to balance the main course; and 'common ground' work shared by all sixth formers. All should continue some training in 'numeracy' and 'literacy' —i.e. some understanding of the language of science and some ability to 'think quantitatively', along with a capacity to speak, write and comprehend argument, and an acquaintance with great writers so as to develop 'a sound social and moral judgment' (Crowther, 270-5). This meant giving arts sixth-formers as much work in science and mathematics as scientists had long been given on the arts side.

With sixth-form general studies so much under pressure from specialist work, a great deal has been left to the conscience of individual schools. Often they have been the extras thrown in after the main subjects have devoured most of the time-table. Less obviously useful, they may be mere 'lip service to a fashionable anxiety', lacking books, time and status (Smith & Lister, 1963). The feeling that this was so led in 1961 to the Agreement to Broaden the Curriculum, a pledge by 360 schools to maintain a full range of subjects up to the sixth-form stage, avoid any total separation of arts and science, and keep at least a third of

83

the sixth-form timetable for non-specialist work. A mass declaration of intent was necessary to prevent schools going it alone from 'martyring' their pupils in the 'university stakes'. A more lasting reaction to the problem was the formation in the following year of the General Studies Association, intended to stimulate interest and publish regular reports of what schools were doing in this field. Its bulletins reflect a widespread emphasis on current affairs, religious and moral problems, the place of science in modern society, and on practical work in art and craft; tutorial groups tend to cut across normal subject divisions. The more socially mixed intake into sixth forms has heightened anxiety about the neglect of general studies. Many may be losing precisely what their homes cannot supply, so that schools have an even greater responsibility for stimulating powers of self-expression, appreciation of the arts, and a taste for reading (Crowther, 1959, 207).

If general studies are to receive more time and status, must they be examined? If they are, the freedom to experiment will be restricted. If they are not, they will be taken lightly by those preoccupied by the hunt for qualifications. The weight of opinion has been very much against increasing the proportion of sixth-form work subject to external examination. But an early attempt to provide an examination without prescribing a syllabus was the General Studies papers introduced by the Northern Board in 1957. These included essay questions on cultural, social, scientific and political topics, together with tests of comprehension, verbal and statistical reasoning, and skill in a foreign language. Cramming for them was claimed to be impossible (Oliver, 1955 & 1957). Other examining boards now set general papers, while some universities accept A-level General Studies in place of O-level qualifications. But doubts remain about the external examining of such work. There

THE SIXTH-FORM CURRICULUM

have been alternative suggestions that universities might show a serious interest in it at interviews, or might ask for its assessment by representatives of a school's examining board or its local institute of education. The logistic difficulties of doing this are obvious. There is a further doubt about the whole value of general studies as traditionally provided—i.e. as minority time on the fringes of the main course. It might simply bolster up a system inherently bad, tackling surface difficulties when the basic defects remain.

The reforming of the sixth-form curriculum

In 1928, the S.S.E.C. proposed an intermediate Higher Certificate because the existing examination was proving too difficult and too specialized for many sixth formers. Something like it has been pursued unsuccessfully ever since. But discussion has been particularly keen in recent years, with doubts about specialization reinforced by rising standards at university entry, the swing from science, and the growing number of sixth formers not taking A-levels at all.

The number of general courses declined still further during the 1950s, and the less academic sixth former was pushed into the common mould of three main subjects. Staying on at school needed some clear goal at the end, and in practice the G.C.E. offered little variety. Few combined work at O- and A-level unless making up an inadequate performance at 16. The old Subsidiary level disappeared. And since the new Scholarship level was used only to select state scholars, the main sixth-form examination was still a leaving examination *and* a means of university selection. Suggestions for some additional test for university applicants which would relieve pressure on other sixth formers produced only the inadequate Special Papers already mentioned. In 1956 the Northern Board suggested an intermediate or general level between O and A for those sixth formers leaving school for employment, often after only one year. This was rejected by the S.S.E.C. because it would attract many who 'ought to aim higher', and bring serious timetabling problems to the schools (S.S.E.C. 1960, 5). In the early 1960s suggestions for combinations of 'full' and 'half' subjects as a way of meeting the variety of sixth-form needs were very much in the air. And the sixth-form curriculum was given priority in the Schools Council programme because the whole nature of sixth forms was changing so fast. The crucial change was the growing number entering sixth forms who did not want or were unsuited to courses of the traditional kind. This was especially true in comprehensive schools, where by 1966 as many as half the sixth form might be taking no A-levels and where some had few or no O-level passes behind them. It was difficult to see how they could be provided for within the G.C.E. framework.

The Schools' Council Working Paper No. 5 (1966) launched a debate which still continues. It called for a pattern flexible enough for courses 'varying in depth and emphasis according to different needs'. A common programme of general studies should provide the focus for all sixth-form work. There should then be a wide range of subjects with 'major' and 'minor' courses offered in each, taking eight or four periods a week. The future university entrant might take two majors and two minors to support or contrast with his specialist work. Other sixth formers might be better served by a larger number of minor courses and no intensive work. Further proposals a year later (S.C. Working Paper 16) retained the idea of only two main subjects, but replaced 'minor' subjects with 'elective' courses which could reflect the location, special needs, and teaching strength of individual schools. These would be internally examined, subject to some form of outside assessment. They might either supplement specialist work, or provide in themselves general courses lasting one or two years. Within this pattern all needs could be met, from the academic high flier to the sixth former simply wanting to go some way beyond O-level or C.S.E.

These proposals were received with suspicion. A committee of headmasters agreed that sixth forms must offer 'every degree of variation' between breadth and depth, but thought this best done through a separate Intermediate examination, subjects at this 'I-level' making the same intellectual demands but covering much less ground It could then provide a focus for the first year of a full A-level course, or a complete one- or two-year course of a less specialized kind (H.M.A., 1968, 52). The universities' response was crucial, since no reform could succeed unless they changed their entry requirements. But they were almost unanimously against any restriction of the number of main subjects to two. This would only increase specialization and continue the premature division between arts and science. 'Elective' courses were thought unlikely to provide an adequate preparation for university study, and impossible to assess for comparability without external examination. What was proposed instead was a pattern of four or five equal two-year courses, preferably including both arts and science subjects. Drastic revision of syllabuses would obviously be necessary to avoid even worse examination pressure and cramming. This new emphasis on breadth at the expense of depth would keep the options open, suiting those who were not yet so subject-minded that they had found the firm centre of their academic interest.

The discussion has been intensive and wide ranging, challenging many traditional assumptions about sixth-form work. What is needed now, perhaps, is a series of experiments in different kinds of sixth-form course in willing schools, with universities and other interested parties prepared to give special consideration to their pupils to avoid any risk to their prospects. Certainly there is almost total agreement on the need for change. 'Study in depth' has had its triumphs. But it is unsuited to the needs of a growing proportion of sixth formers, and to the present rapid expansion in 'upper secondary' schooling.

6
Growth and change

In *'L'Explosion Scolaire'*, Cros argues that educational institutions are everywhere breaking up under the pressure
of numbers and new needs. 'Physical phenomena often
change their nature when they change their scale; human
phenomena do the same.' Analogies with the physical
world are rarely helpful, but it may well be that the English
sixth form, so deeply rooted in the past, has now gone
beyond mere adaptation to change. Some drastic recon-
struction may be needed. In 1912 there were 9,500 sixth
formers in grant-aided schools. The increase to almost
40,000 in 1938 involved no great changes in organization
or curriculum. In 1958 there were 70,000, and in 1966, over
170,000. Even within grammar schools, the implications
of growth on this scale are far reaching. But a far greater
challenge to tradition has come from the development of
advanced work outside them.

Teachers and teaching methods

Sixth-form teaching has long been seen as the 'joy and
reward' of grammar school work, the 'charm of the whole
business'. Here, at least in theory, the students are willing,
standards are high, and the teachers able to give full rein

to their academic knowledge and enthusiasm. If university entrants are to be a year or more ahead of their contemporaries in other countries, then schools must have 'a core of academic specialists able to talk on the level with their colleagues at the next stage' (Reeves, 1965, 158). This need and reputation for 'scholarship' are important reasons for the attraction of sixth-form teaching. So is the association of professional status with the age of those taught and the degree of specialization involved. It is not surprising, then, that so much hostility to sixth-form colleges comes from those threatened with the loss of advanced work or with a sharp choice between it and main-school teaching.

Large sixth forms often mean higher salaries, not only because older pupils are worth so many extra units to their school's grade, but also because special responsibility allowances are frequently tied to A-level teaching. The original advanced course grants of 1917 had provided money for books, equipment, and a salary well within the existing range. There was no suggestion that sixth-form work be rewarded at a special rate. And particularly in the 1930s, well qualified graduates were so easy to recruit that no financial bait was needed. It was the introduction of special responsibility allowances in 1945 which brought clear opportunities for rewarding advanced teaching. Ten years later the Burnham Committee recommended that anyone taking more than five periods a week beyond O-level was to get an allowance. Though likely to lead to some clever juggling with individual time-tables, the move was welcomed as 'recognizing the importance of sixth-form work in the national economy' (T.E.S., 4 March 1955, 234). It was also open to attack as creating a hierarchy of teachers, ignoring other ways of contributing to school life, and distracting attention from securing a decent basic salary. And through the continuing argument over differentials have run references to a separate 'grammar school scale'. Thus a survey in 1958 showed 75 per cent grammar school teachers with special allowances compared with 60 per cent in technical schools and only 40 per cent in secondary moderns (*T.E.S.*, 4 April 1958, 544). Since that time, comprehensive reorganization has increased the number of 'organizational posts'—e.g. heads of house, heads of middle school, year masters. But within subject departments, allowances are still tied closely to the more academic work.

With so much talk of 'professional unemployment', the 1930s brought a buyers' market for graduates. Twenty years later, there were already loud complaints from schools of having to frame courses to the staff available, and starve junior forms to feed the sixth. In science, with so many alternatives open to graduates, the shortage became acute. Desperate expedients were suggested, such as a period of compulsory teaching for all those with science degrees, and the first large group excused National Service were those 'good graduates' in mathematics and science appointed to schools doing advanced work. It was a deteriorating situation. The proportion of teachers with good degrees was markedly higher among the over-40s, while the schools were recruiting a far higher proportion of 'other degrees' than were industry, commerce, local government or the Civil Service (Crowther, 1959, 233-8). Crowther himself described the section on teacher supply as 'the most frightening part' of his Report. Girls' schools especially were finding it so hard to make appointments in science that 'they will soon be able to recruit a physics graduate only once every forty years and a good honours degree every hundred' (D.E.S. *Statistics of Education*, 1962, Part I, 65). Certainly recruitment fell far behind the rise in sixth-form numbers. In 1965, for example, the number of chemistry graduates entering university training departments was 3 per cent down on 1962 and the number of physics graduates 15 per cent down; in the same years the number of A-level passes in the two subjects increased by 12 per cent and 20 per cent.

The worst fears about declining quality have not been realized, for the proportion of 'good degrees' among recent graduate recruits has actually increased, especially in science. But lack of numbers remains an urgent problem, heightened by the multiplying opportunities for teachers in technical colleges and colleges of education. Effects on the schools are obvious. Many sixth-form groups become too large to handle in discussion or laboratory work. Main school classes stay large because sixth forms take far more than their 'share' of staff time. Many specialists are forced to concentrate almost entirely on A-level work at the expense of other teaching, and a reason often given for the swing from science is that some make their crucial choice of subjects without having been taught at all by real specialists in mathematics or science. The shortage reinforces arguments for the concentration of staff in sixth-form centres, and for radical changes in teaching method.

The sixth form has traditionally been distinguished by a particular style of teaching, a close relationship between teacher and taught. This reflects the eagerness of voluntary pupils to study their chosen subjects, and the role of the sixth form as the bridge to the university. It is a time when 'school discipline fades into the background, when instruction becomes study'. The emphasis now is on discussion, independent work, a free exchange of ideas with the teacher as catalyst.

This is the ideal. It may well over-dramatize the break between main school and sixth form, excusing arid methods at O-level for the sake of the glory to come. And it may collapse in practice before the pressure to show results in terms of scholarships, university places and high grades. Many sixth formers will be less 'intellectual disciples' than hard-headed pursuers of qualifications (they may, of course, be both). Teachers may feel torn between those methods they think right, and those 'relentless examination techniques' which apparently guarantee results. Too much time may be given to the main subjects, and too much direct teaching done within them. General studies and private study are the obvious casualties. The value of independent work at this stage is apparent. Yet surveys have shown marked differences between schools in the time allowed for it. Some lack room to accommodate private study. Some encourage the taking of four A-levels which consume most of the timetable, or allow 8-10 periods a week to each of the three main subjects.

Official advice on sixth-form teaching usually assumes small numbers and an intimate contact between teacher and student. This was easily provided in the 1930s, when a few chairs around a table or a part of a laboratory was often all the special provision necessary. Now the sheer organization of sixth-form work is a major problem. In 1956, at the beginning of the 'explosion' in numbers, the I.A.A.M. urged that twenty should be the maximum size for any sixth-form class. In 1966 over 25 per cent of sixth formers were in classes larger than this, and 10 per cent were being taught in groups of over 30. The result of large classes is often an uneasy compromise between lecture and seminar which achieves the aims of neither. At least in large schools, setting within main subject groups invites experiments in team teaching at this level. But in many schools, it is impossible to provide adequate advanced teaching in the traditional framework of classrooms of roughly equal size. There is a need for lecture halls, since a lecture may as well be given to 100 as to 30; for small seminar rooms; for independent study booths; for easier use of films, tapes and television to reinforce overworked staff. This suggests accommodation quite different and separate from the main secondary school (D.E.S. Building Bulletins 16 & 41).

The sixth form within the school

'The sixth form is indeed the most characteristic and most valuable feature in a grammar school in the training of character and a sense of responsibility, and on its existence depends all that is best in the grammar school tradition. Not only does it make possible that free and ordered self-government that is the admiration and envy of educationists of other lands, but it acts as a perpetual stimulus to the work of both teacher and pupil.' This eulogy from the Spens Report is a fine example of the virtues traditionally ascribed to the sixth form, as a leaven out of all proportion to its size, the main source of standards in work, behaviour and play. Academically it has represented the role of grammar schools as the path to higher education. Socially it has served as a 'training ground for leaders' and a convenient reinforcement in the day-to-day running of the schools.

Prefects became indispensable aides in the short-staffed schools of Thomas Arnold's day. They were also seen as deriving great benefit themselves from their exercise of authority. Strongly established and extolled in the public schools, the prefect system was generally imitated in the grammar schools, and at least until the 1930s there were few articulate critics. But in recent years criticism has mounted. The prefect system has been blamed for creating an unnecessary gulf between sixth and fifth forms, turning sixth formers into unpaid assistants in return for trifling privileges and uncertain status. It may be true that 'the senior boy, accorded official status by the community, put his energies into tasks of social leadership; he didn't have to prove his authority by bullying, fighting, or other forms of anti-social behaviour' (Wilkinson, 1964, 31). But authority bestowed from above and resting on obvious differences in maturity has been attacked as more suitable to an Empire full of subject peoples than to a society dependent on influence over equals and supposedly open to mass participation in the making of decisions (Eckstein, 1966, 188).

Fascinating as the link may be between school prefects and the decline of the British Empire, more mundane facts challenge the 'élitist' aspects of the prefect system. When sixth forms were small, their members were obviously leaders of the school and posts of responsibility were easily shared. When they are large, can prefects be chosen fairly when the position has possible advantages in university and career selection? Should prefects be elected, or the duties shared out among the entire sixth form? Will pupils accept *orders* from near-contemporaries? And, a more basic question, do sixth formers any longer need or want this responsibility for their juniors? For with larger numbers has come earlier sophistication. In some ways, sixth formers are more young adults than they have been in the past. Can they still be contained within the atmosphere thought right for their juniors? Schools with pupils 11-18 cover a much wider age range than does any other stage in the educational system, and the presence of young children may involve 'a paternalism in discipline which often spreads upwards to those who do not need it' (Crowther, 1959, 411). If the sixth form is almost 'a society in its own right', how separate should it be? A sense of separation is apparent in the magazine *Sixth Form Opinion*, and is recognized in the growing provision of sixth-form common rooms. It is accepted with approval in two imaginative bulletins on sixth-form accommodation issued by the D.E.S. in 1965 and 1967. 'Incentives to remain at school will be stronger if the environment provided for these older pupils, both in quantity and quality, acknowledges their status as young adults' (Bulletin, 25, 1965, 1). Of course, some degree of separation is possible within a full secondary school. At High Wycombe girls' grammar school, for example, sixth formers in 1965 were wearing no uniform, holding their own assemblies, having considerable freedom to organize their work, and were able to choose whether or not to participate in the social life of the rest of the school because prefects were chosen from outside its ranks. But they still shared the same buildings and facilities. Plans for changes more radical than this are discussed later in the chapter.

Sixth forms with a difference

In the years after 1944 the Ministry of Education supported and even reinforced the selective and academic character of grammar schools. Their aim was to be a continuous seven-year course for most of their pupils. At the same time, technical schools were slow to develop, while secondary moderns were shielded from the pressures, and rewards, of external examinations. Overlapping between the three prongs of the tripartite system was inevitable. Grammar school teachers themselves wanted a broader curriculum than was suggested for them. With transfers to grammar schools far less frequent than 'mistakes' in selection, secondary modern schools insisted on preparing some of their pupils for those qualifications necessary for white collar employment. A few began extended courses beyond O-level. In technical schools, sixth forms appeared offering a full range of subjects. Even so, 95 per cent of all 17-year-olds at school in 1958 were in independent or state-aided grammar schools, and the alternative route to higher education remained very narrow.

In that year, half the technical schools had sixth forms, and it was suggested in the Crowther Report that they were well suited to take transfers from secondary modern schools at 16+, especially where the parents had little experience of prolonged education and might be put off by the 'high' academic atmosphere of a grammar school. Certainly, many of their courses had an obvious vocational purpose, the Associated Examining Board having been set up in 1954 to cover normally neglected technical and commercial subjects. Their sixth forms could therefore be described as wider in scope, less bound to university requirements and so under less intense pressure, and as more satisfying to many students because a vocational target was clearly in sight (Edwards, 1960, 142). A far higher proportion went on to technical colleges than to universities, and direct entry into employment was commoner than from grammar school sixth forms. Important as these differences are, it must be remembered that the tripartite system has never existed in more than name because technical schools have been so few. Only 3,000 18-year-olds left them in 1965-6 compared with 52,000 from grammar schools.

In the summer examinations of 1966, there were over 3,000 A-level candidates from secondary modern schools. This shows how far the limits put on their work after 1944 have been exceeded. It also suggests some highly un-economic advanced teaching. Against the advantages of providing sixth-form courses within a familiar environment must be set the 'extravagant waste' of teachers' time on sets

97

of two or three students. This argument has long been heard in the debate on comprehensive education. The main doubt about multilateral schools in the Spens Report (1938) was that an unselected intake would have to be so large to provide a viable sixth form as to make the whole school quite unmanageable. This point was made again and again during the years 1945-7 in defence of the grammar schools. The spectre of 10-11 stream entries was conjured up, since anything smaller would deny equality of opportunity to the ablest by providing too narrow a choice of subjects. When the Middlesex authority in 1948 announced 1,000 as the maximum size for its comprehensives, it was thought to have set itself an insoluble problem of sixth-form organization.

Supporters of comprehensive schooling were bound to play the grammar schools at their own game, and to advertise their academic successes, for example, the 45 passes, 9 county awards and 3 state scholarships gained by 19 A-level entrants from Holyhead County School in 1953 (Pedley, 1956, 10). But the extremely slow introduction of such schools made it difficult to judge whether their ablest pupils were being held back. Even in 1959 no comprehensive school had sixth formers completing an advanced course who had been there since the age of 11. An L.C.C. Report two years later rejected any idea of a decline in standards, noting the large sixth forms in some of its comprehensives (for instance, 150 in Wandsworth School), the reasonable number in some with 'poor' 11-plus intakes, and the exceptionally wide range of courses being offered. Another survey by the I.A.A.M., an association dominated by grammar school teachers, was also optimistic : 'Let it be said that the comprehensive school does well by its intellectual cream in the sixth form . . .' (A.M.A., 1960, 32). Yet doubts have remained. 'In England our selective system, whatever its faults may be, has developed in the sixth form an academic training of outstanding merit. We have now deliberately turned our backs on selection. . . . Can the standard of the sixth form be maintained in a comprehensive system?' (Fisher, 1967, 7). The same question was asked by twenty-five university heads in a joint letter to *The Times*. They saw a threat to academic standards in hasty and ill-prepared schemes of comprehensive reorganization, and especially in 'the diffusion of specialist staff' (3 June 1967).

The facts of the situation provide ammunition for both sides. An extensive survey in 1965 showed the average number of sixth formers in comprehensive schools as 75; 11 per cent of the schools covered had fewer than 25, 40 per cent had fewer than 50, and 22 per cent more than 100. But many of those with small sixth forms were in rural areas where the grammar schools they replaced had fared even worse. Others were only beginning advanced work, or had less than their share of able pupils (Monks, 1968, 34-6). The average size of grammar school sixth forms in 1965 was 110. But there were still 77 schools with fewer than 300 pupils and 263 with fewer than 400. Clearly, some comprehensives concentrate work previously scattered over several small schools, and avoid a skeleton development of advanced work in secondary moderns. Estimates of a sufficient intake to provide a viable sixth form often ignore the effect of comprehensive education itself on the wish to stay on, and of the (apparently) imminent raising of the school leaving age. Comparison of A-level results add nothing to the argument, because comprehensive school sixth forms have a wider academic range and include a growing proportion not doing A-level work—a proportion as high as 37 per cent in a 1966 sample of Inner London comprehensive schools.

Leavers from secondary schools aged 18 and over, 1965-6

	Took no A-levels	Failed all	Passed 1	2	3	4
Grammar	5%	9%	17%	25%	37%	8%
Technical	5	9	27	23	27	8
Comprehensive	17	13	18	20	26	5

Indeed, the variety of sixth-form work offered increases the proportion wanting to stay on. The *A.M.A.* report already quoted claimed that instead of fitting pupils to courses, the comprehensive schools worked the other way round—the largest being able to give pupils 'any course they need' (*A.M.A.*, 1960, 33). Their intake is now so varied in background, achievement and need that the 1917 definition of sixth formers as those doing work *beyond* School Certificate level has become obsolete.

'A growing sixth form is inevitably a sixth form with a widening range of ability and an increasing diversity of educational needs' (S.C. Working Paper 5, 12). It is obvious that to provide for 'every variety of breadth and depth' must be more expensive in staff than the traditional academic pattern. The whole concept of 'viability' in sixth-form work has therefore to be revised. In the 1930s, sixth forms of 30-40 were quite acceptable; recent discussion of the 'right' size for an all-through comprehensive has tended to work from a sixth-form figure of at least 150; a full range of academic, general and vocational courses may need far larger numbers. Such calculations reinforce the common hostility to large schools, and the growing feeling that older children may benefit from a separate environment. The result has been proposals for a complete re-shaping of secondary education, replacing a unified second stage with a tiered system based on 'middle schools' (9-13 years) or some pattern of junior and senior high schools, or else the concentration of sixth-form work in certain schools and separate centres.

Sixth-form centres and sixth-form colleges

Considering this 'increasing diversity of educational needs', the Crowther Committee called for larger catchment areas for those institutions providing full-time education beyond the minimum school leaving age. An adequate choice of course was only possible if pupils were brought to the teachers, transferring them if necessary to schools where the 'centre of gravity' would lie with this older age group (Crowther, 1959, 417). The idea was not new. Early this century, large grammar schools often took 16-year-olds from neighbouring schools unable to provide advanced work, and the Board of Education repeatedly urged the avoidance of wasteful duplication through planning sixth-form courses by area rather than by individual school. More recently, many secondary modern pupils have gone on to technical and grammar schools, while some boarding accommodation has been provided in rural areas for those whose specialist needs could not be met within reach of their homes. Such transfers have normally meant only absorbing a few extra into a well-established sixth form. What is emerging now is the concentration of pupils from a number of schools, either in a bloc attached to one of them or in a separate 'college'. The first alternative creates an 'expanded sixth form', perhaps temporarily expanded until the feeder schools develop sixth forms of their own. At Mexborough in Yorkshire, for example, the sixth form moved into specially designed premises in September 1964, though some facilities and staff were shared with the lower school. By 1968, 192 of the 433 sixth formers had come in at 16, most of them from seven secondary modern schools in the area. It was intended from the beginning to free the sixth form from any close connection with the lower school, reduce rules to a minimum, and make it largely self-governing through an elected council. Social life centres on a common room open all day and some evenings, the considerable profits from a snack bar being entirely at the disposal of the students. Very few sixth formers are prefects, contact with the lower school being maintained largely through games and societies. One headmaster is still responsible for the whole age range 11-18. A similar centre was built, with great attention to detail, at Rosebery County Secondary School in Epsom. In 1966, half its 300 sixth formers had entered the school at 16. Accommodation and atmosphere were designed to advertise their status as 'young adults'. Teaching space was divided into lecture hall, seminar rooms and small study booths, and much of the work was unsupervised. The large common room was to look as little like the traditional school room as possible. It included coffee bar and self-service cafeteria, and was open in the evenings. There was no uniform. The whole bloc was sited so that younger pupils could get tempting glimpses of the attractions of sixth-form life (D.E.S. Building Bulletin 41, 1967).

In both these examples, some links with a lower school were retained. A completely separate sixth-form college represents a more radical break with tradition. It has therefore 'met the abuse commonly reserved for blasphemy' (*T.E.S.*, 19 February 1965, 514). Serious debate began in 1955 when the Croydon education authority published its Addington College plan. Over half the sixth-form teaching groups in the area at that time had fewer than five students. To gather them all under one roof would enable the authority to 'rival the public schools in library facilities, equipment and well qualified staff', while also providing a setting adult enough to remove the social handicap of being at school while contemporaries were at work. The plan was bitterly attacked by local grammar school teachers, and rejected by an outside expert called in to vet it. A revised plan in 1962 was approved by a new expert, but local attacks were no less fierce. Croydon is still without its college, but the idea is now a major issue in comprehensive reorganization.

Given the strength of traditional ideas about the value of sixth forms, the opposition is predictable. Schools would lose their leaders, and sixth formers their opportunities to lead—a curious argument, since the chance to take responsibility is simply brought forward, and new leaders are found wherever the top of the school happens to be. A college may involve too much freedom, offering 'immature minds a pseudo-adult atmosphere . . . the student will no longer be conscious of himself as part of a community with a position to enjoy and duties to perform. A system of graduated privilege and responsibility *within* the context of a school provides the necessary emancipation and a desirable continuity' (*A.M.A.*, May 1965, 151). A move at sixteen away from a familiar environment would be unsettling, discouraging many from staying on by depriving them of support at a time of crucial decisions for courses and future careers; the whole idea was therefore 'badly conceived from a psycho-social point of view' (Miller, 1964). Those teaching advanced work were likely for that very reason to be more stimulating with younger pupils. They should not be separated from them, or forced to lose contact with the early learning of their subjects. This argument can be taken too far, for pressure of sixth-form work already excludes many from junior teaching, while some teachers might combine work at a college and at a nearby school. But continuity in syllabus and approach are difficult where the feeder schools are widely scattered. This makes the arrangement at Banbury an attractive one, with schools and their 'centre for advanced education' sharing the same site.

Many of these arguments can be stood on their head, with no evidence as yet to confute or confirm them. Of the 236 comprehensive plans submitted by the end of 1967, only 24 included sixth-form colleges and another 39 sixth-form centres attached to existing secondary schools. Colleges are now going ahead in a number of areas, but that at Luton offers one of very few working models. Some see this break at 16 as more natural than a move to a senior high school a year or two earlier, because it allows a longer main school course. A move to a new and freer atmosphere may persuade some doubters to stay on, and technical colleges have long been used to recruiting at that age. The 'economic' advantages of concentration may seem obvious, with staff and resources brought together where they can be used most intensively. Yet the colleges would have to be large—perhaps 500 or more—to make full use of specialist teachers who were not also working below that level. Many teachers deprived of the stimulus of advanced work, 'the reward earned by hard labour lower down the school', might be lost to the schools altogether (A.M.A., 1967, 112). But it has also been argued that since graduates tend to see themselves very much as teachers of subjects, the all-through comprehensive so dilutes this instructional role with more general and pastoral work as to make it far less attractive to them. Sixth-form colleges, however, might match in status and specialized work the many opportunities for graduates in further education and teacher training (Bernbaum, 1967, 163).

The sixth form and further education

Sixth-form colleges have been praised as the best compromise between postponing selection and preserving standards of academic excellence. They have been attacked as incompatible with a truly comprehensive system because they merely delay the separation of the academic from the non-academic. Obviously, the colleges can develop in very different ways. Croydon's Addington College was intended to concentrate on A-level courses. The Sixth-Form College at Luton emphasizes them sufficiently to exclude some applicants not thought suitable for academic work; this is because other types of course are available in the area high schools or in the College of Technology. Such a plan might mean withdrawing A-level courses from the local college of further education, leaving it less comprehensive than at present. But an overwhelmingly academic sixth form is becoming untenable in many grammar schools, and is being actively rejected in comprehensive schools. Alternatively, sixth formers can be absorbed into something like the American junior college, offering a wide variety of course to a restricted age range. Experiments in this direction were recommended in the Crowther Report: 'What we have in mind is an institution with an adult atmosphere of a technical college, but with a much wider range of curriculum and with terms of reference nearer to those of a school, in that equal weight would be attached by the staff to the subjects taught and the individual development of the student' (422). It would take full-time students only. This is very much the pattern at Mexborough, where the college is open to all who wish to take a course 'whatever their previous educational history and qualifications', and where the work can be directed to A-level, O-level, some vocational goal, or be without any immediate examination objective. The headmaster comments that such breadth was easier to provide because the college was 'not to any great extent in competition with technical education provided by the West

Riding', and it is easy to see how demarcation disputes could arise. A policy statement by the Association of Teachers in Technical Institutions (1966) suggested that all 'vocationally committed' work should be left to the technical colleges. But such commitment would be very hard to define, and the present overlap is wide. Schools offer courses in, for example, technical drawing, metalwork and commercial subjects, while a quarter of all A-level entries in 1966 came from technical colleges, many of them in arts and pure science.

A third solution is the fusion of sixth form and further education. This would be a most radical change. Sixth forms have long provided an academic training for the small minority heading towards the universities and the professions. Though those leaving school at 15 or 16 have been increasingly able to follow the 'alternative route' of full-time or part-time courses in technical colleges, there has been little or no contact between the two groups. In a book on comprehensive education, published in 1956, Robin Pedley argued the case for bringing together all those aged 15-18 into county colleges, where they could mix freely during 'perhaps the most vital years of all in the formation of social attitudes'. Until recently, the idea received little serious consideration. Circular 5/65 urged local authorities to study the needs of this age group as a whole to avoid duplication, but the directive was broad and vague. The rapid development of A-level courses in technical colleges and of general and vocational work in sixth forms has reinforced the case for fusion. In several places, for example in Exeter and Barnstaple, plans for comprehensive reorganization include the transfer of all sixth-form work to the local technical colleges. It is claimed that this would mean the maximum use of resources, and would end divisions between academic and technical, full-time and part-time, study.

The plans have met bitter opposition, and they certainly involve formidable problems. Schools and colleges have developed along very different lines, they are administered separately, their staffs are recruited and paid according to very different standards. The colleges have generally lacked that emphasis on sport, pastoral care and 'community spirit' associated with sixth forms, and 'liberal studies' tend to have a low status not found in schools. But these are local solutions to the challenge of comprehensive reorganization. Sixth-form work will long continue to be organized in many different ways—in colleges and centres, in senior high schools, in all-through grammar and comprehensive schools. And for all the changes outlined in this book, it must be remembered that 'full-time secondary education extending over seven years is still a minority experience: what we have been seeing . . . is a marked increase in the size of that minority' (S.C. Working Paper 16, 20). What is happening in the sixth forms of some comprehensive schools and in such places as Mexborough is a long stride away from the tradition of retaining at school only a minority on whom stringent academic demands can be made. The American junior colleges began life as preparatory departments for the universities. They came to offer a complete range of academic, vocational and general work to a large majority of the age-group. This country may be moving slowly in the same direction, making the years 16-18 a natural 'third' stage of education.

Suggestions for further reading

General

There is no detailed overall survey of the development of
sixth forms. The most comprehensive account is Part 5 of
the Crowther Report (1959). This might be followed up
by comparing official recommendations on sixth-form work
over a long period—e.g. *Memoranda on Teaching and
Organization in Secondary Schools* (Board of Education,
1913), *The Organization and Curriculum of Sixth Forms*
(Board of Education, 1939), *The Road to the Sixth Form*
(Ministry of Education, 1951), and the Schools Council
Working Paper No. 5. There is a most useful comparative
study in Spolton, L., *The Upper Secondary School* (Pergamon, 1967). Two very recent publications are Morris, N.,
Sixth Form to College Entrance (Routledge & Kegan Paul,
1969), and King, R. W., *The English Sixth-Form College*
(Pergamon, 1969). The *Times Educational Supplement* produced a special survey of sixth forms in 1949, and there is
an account of advanced work in a hundred North country
grammar schools in *Trends in Education No. 7* (Department
of Education and Science, 1967). Useful references to the
work and 'ethos' of sixth forms can be found in more
general studies of grammar schools, e.g. those by Harry
Davies and Frances Stevens listed in the references; Hutchinson, M., and Young, C., *Educating the Intelligent* (Penguin,
1965); and Davies, R., *The Grammar School* (Penguin, 1967).

Curriculum and examinations

The sixth-form curriculum before 1944 must be studied

mainly through official reports and in the various educational journals. More recently there have been some useful surveys, e.g. Association for Education in Citizenship, *Sixth Form Citizens* (O.U.P., 1950); Oxford University Education Department, *Arts and Science in the Sixth Form* (1960) and *Technology and the Sixth-Form Boy* (1963); the Leverhulme Study Group, *The Complete Scientist* (O.U.P., 1961). The present debate about specialization can be followed through the Crowther Report, the third and sixth *Reports* of the Secondary School Examinations Council (1960 and 1962), Schools Council *Working Papers* 5 (1965) and *16* (1967), and the Headmasters' Association pamphlet *The Sixth Form of the Future* (1968).

The development of examinations at sixth-form level can be seen in Petch, J. A., *Fifty Years of Examining* (Harrap, 1953); Jeffrey, G. B. (editor), *External Examinations in Secondary Schools* (Harrap, 1958); Wiseman, S. (editor), *Examinations in English Education* (Manchester University Press, 1961); and Montgomery, R. J., *Examinations* (Longmans, 1965).

The sixth form to university

There are useful accounts of the problems of university selection and the competition for places in Dale, R. R., *From School to University* (Routledge & Kegan Paul, 1954); Furneaux, W. D., *The Chosen Few* (O.U.P., 1961); and Reeves, M. (editor), *Eighteen-Plus* (Faber, 1965); also the articles by Himmelweit, H., and Kelsall, R., in *Sociological Review Monograph* No. 7, 1963. The 'accuracy' of university selection methods are discussed in the articles by Albrow, M. C. and Oliver, R. A. C., listed in the references. The university point of view can be examined in various reports by the Standing Conference on University Entry.

The sixth form and the reorganization of secondary education

The development of sixth-form work outside the grammar schools is described in the books by Reese Edwards, Robin Pedley and T. G. Monks, and in the reports by the London County Council (1961) and the Assistant Masters' Association (1960 and 1967)—all listed in the references. See also: Pedley, R., *The Comprehensive School* (Penguin, 1963); Cole, R., *The Comprehensive School in Action* (Oldbourne, 1964); The National Association of Schoolmasters, *The Comprehensive School* (1964). The variety of provision for sixth-form work in schemes of comprehensive re-organization appears clearly in Maclure, S. (editor), *Comprehensive Planning* (Councils and Education Press, 1965), and in the policy statement by the Association of Teachers in Technical Institutions, *The Organization of Secondary Education* (1966).

The cases for and against sixth-form colleges can be found in the first report by the Croydon Education Committee on the Addington College plan (1955); the National Union of Teachers discussion document *Sixth Form Colleges* (1966), the report in the *A.M.A.*, Vol. 60, No. 4 (May 1965), and in Corbett, Anne, *Sixth Form Colleges* (New Society, 28 March 1968). For descriptions of sixth-form centres and colleges from the inside see: Shield, G. W., *A Sixth Form College at Work* (*Education*, 6 November, 1964); Dance, B. D., *Living and Working in a Sixth-Form College* (*Times Educational Supplement*, 21 August 1967); and D.E.S. Building Bulletin No. 41, *Sixth Form Centre* (1967).

Bibliography

ALBROW, M. C. (1967), 'Ritual and Reason in the Selection of Students', *Universities Quarterly*, Vol. 21, No. 2.

ARMYTAGE, W. H. G. (1958), 'Education and Energy Slaves', in *World Year Book of Education*, Evans.

ASSISTANT MASTERS ASSOCIATION (1960), *Teaching in Comprehensive Schools*, Cambridge University Press.

   (1967), *Teaching in Comprehensive Schools: a Second Report*, Cambridge University Press.

   (1965), 'Sixth Form Colleges', *A.M.A.*, Vol. 60, No. 4, May.

ASSISTANT MISTRESSES ASSOCIATION (1939), *Memorandum on Sixth Form Life and Work in Girls' Secondary Schools*, University of London Press.

BANKS, O. L. (1955), *Parity and Prestige in English Secondary Education*, Routledge & Kegan Paul.

BERNBAUM, G. (1967), 'Educational Expansion and the Teacher's Role', *Universities Quarterly*, Vol. 21, No. 2.

BOARD OF EDUCATION: Annual Reports on Education.

   (1911), Report of the Consultative Committee: *Examinations in Secondary Schools*, H.M.S.O.

   (1913), *Memoranda on Teaching and Organization in Secondary Schools*, H.M.S.O.

   (1913), Circular No. 1023, H.M.S.O.

   (1926), Report of the Consultative Committee: *The Education of the Adolescent* (Hadow Report), H.M.S.O.

   (1926), *Statistics*, H.M.S.O.

   (1938), Report of the Consultative Committee: *Secondary Education* (Spens Report), H.M.S.O.

(1939), *The Organization and Curriculum of Sixth Forms in Secondary Schools*, Pamphlet No. 114, H.M.S.O.

(1943), Report of the Committee of the Secondary School Examinations Council : *Curriculum and Examinations in Secondary Schools* (Norwood Report), H.M.S.O.

BRITISH ASSOCIATION FOR THE ADVANCEMENT OF SCIENCE (1944), Report of Committee on Post-War University Education. Published by the Association.

BRIGGS, A. (1965), 'Thomas Hughes and the Public Schools', in *Victorian People*, Penguin Books.

BURSTALL, SARA (1907), *English High Schools for Girls*, Longmans.

CLARK, BURTON R. (1961), 'The Cooling Out Function in Higher Education' in Halsey, A. H., Floud, J., Anderson, C. A. (editors), *Education, Economy and Society*, Free Press, New York.

COMMITTEE ON HIGHER EDUCATION (1963), *Higher Education* (Robbins Report), H.M.S.O.

COUNCIL FOR SCIENTIFIC POLICY (1968), *Enquiry into the Flow of Candidates in Science and Technology into Higher Education* (Dainton Report), H.M.S.O.

CROS, L. (1963), *L'Explosion Scolaire*, Sevpen.

COUNTY BOROUGH OF CROYDON (1955), *The Addington College Scheme*, mimeographed for the authority.

(1962), *Secondary Education in Croydon*, mimeographed for the authority.

DAVIES, H. (1945), *The Boys' Grammar School, Today and Tomorrow*, Methuen.

(1965), *Culture and the Grammar School*, Routledge & Kegan Paul.

DEPARTMENT OF EDUCATION AND SCIENCE, Annual *Statistics of Education*, H.M.S.O.

(1965), *Sixth Form and Staff*, Building Bulletin No. 25, H.M.S.O.

(1967), *Sixth Form Centre*, Building Bulletin, No. 41, H.M.S.O.

(1967), *Trends in Education*, No. 7, H.M.S.O.

ECKSTEIN, M. A. (1966), 'The Elitist and the Popular Ideal: Prefects and Monitors in English and American Schools', *International Review of Education*, Vol. 12.

EDWARDS, REESE (1960), *The Secondary Technical School*, University of London Press.

FISHER, F. (1967), 'Comprehension and the Sixth Form', *Conference*, Vol. 4, No. 2.

FLOUD, J. (1954), 'The Educational Experience of the Adult Population' in Glass, D. (editor), *Social Mobility in Britain*, Routledge & Kegan Paul.

FURNEAUX, W. D. (1961), *The Chosen Few*, Oxford University Press.

GRAY, J. L. and MOSHINSKY, P. (1938), 'Ability and Opportunity in English Education' in Hogben, L. (editor), *Political Arithmetic*, Allen & Unwin.

HARVARD REPORT (1946), *General Education in a Free Society*, Harvard University Press.

HEADMASTER'S ASSOCIATION (1968), *The Sixth Form of the Future*, published by the Association.

HIMMELWEIT, H. (1963), 'Student Selection', *Sociological Review* Monograph No. 7.

HOME UNIVERSITIES CONFERENCE (1955), *Report*, printed on behalf of The Association of the Universities of the British Commonwealth.

LAWRENCE, P. (1964), *Advanced-Level and After*, Northern Universities Joint Board.

MACKENZIE, SIR COMPTON (1963), *My Life and Times, Octave 2*, Chatto & Windus.

MILLER, D. (1964), 'Sixth Form Colleges', *New Education*, December.

MILLER, G. W. (1968), 'The Relevance of Dainton to University Entrance', *Times Educational Supplement*, 3 March.

MINISTRY OF EDUCATION (1945), *The Nation's Schools*, Pamphlet No. 1, H.M.S.O.

(1947), *The New Secondary Education*, Pamphlet No 9, H.M.S.O.

(1951), *The Road to the Sixth Form*, Pamphlet No. 19, H.M.S.O.

(1954), Central Advisory Council on Education: Report on *Early Leaving*, H.M.S.O.

(1959), Central Advisory Council on Education. *15-18* (Crowther Report), H.M.S.O.

MINISTRY OF EDUCATION AND THE SCOTTISH EDUCATION DEPARTMENT (1960), *Grants to Students* (Anderson Report), H.M.S.O.

MONKS, T. G. (1968), *Comprehensive Education in England and Wales*, National Foundation for Educational Research.

MONTGOMERY, R. J. (1965), *Examinations: An Account of their Development as Administrative Devices in England*, Longmans.

MOWAT, C. L. (1955), *Britain Between the Wars*, Methuen.

OLIVER, R. A. C. (1955), *An Experimental Examination in General Studies*, Northern Joint Board publication.

(1957), *The Northern Joint Board Examination in General Studies*, Northern Joint Board publication.

(1966), 'University Entrance Requirements: Whence and Whither?', *Universities Quarterly*, Vol. 20, No. 3.

OLLERENSHAW, K. (1961), *The Education of Girls*, Faber.

PEDLEY, R. (1956), *Comprehensive Education: A New Approach*, Gollancz.

PERCY, E. (1958), *Some Memories*, Eyre & Spottiswode.

PETERSON, A. D. C. (1960), *Arts and Science in the Sixth*

Form, Oxford University Department of Education, March.

REEVES, N. (editor), (1965), *Eighteen Plus: Unity and Diversity in Higher Education*, Faber.

ROWSE, A. L. (1942), *A Cornish Childhood*, Cape.

SADLER, M. E. (1903), *Secondary and Higher Education in Sheffield*.

    (1904), *Secondary and Higher Education in Derbyshire*.

    (1905), *Secondary and Higher Education in Essex*.

These reports were produced for local authorities.

SCHOOLS COUNCIL (1966), *The Sixth Form: Curriculum and Examinations*, Working Paper No. 5, H.M.S.O.

    Some Further Proposals for Sixth Form Work, Working Paper No. 16, H.M.S.O.

SECONDARY SCHOOL EXAMINATIONS COUNCIL (1939), *The Higher Certificate*, H.M.S.O.

    (1960), *The G.C.E. and Sixth Form Studies*, H.M.S.O.

    (1962), *Sixth Form Studies and University Entrance Requirements*, H.M.S.O.

SMITH, R. IRVINE, and LISTER, I. (1963), 'The Debate on the Sixth Form Curriculum', *General Studies Association Bulletin*, No. 1.

SPOLTON, L. (1967), *Upper Secondary School: a Comparative Survey*, Pergamon.

STEVENS, F. (1960), *The Living Tradition*, Hutchinson.

UNIVERSITY GRANTS COMMITTEE: regular Reports on University Development, H.M.S.O.

WILKINSON, R. (1964), *The Prefects*, O.U.P.

WILLIAMS, E. (1961), *George*, Hamish Hamilton.